The Power of Prayer, Endurance and Truth

The Power of Prayer, Endurance and Truth

David Beato

The Power of Prayer, Endurance and Truth

Published by Trastevere Publishing

For more information contact:
trasteverebooks@comcast.net

Book design by:
www.arborbooks.com

Printed in the United States of America

The Power of Prayer, Endurance and Truth
David Beato

1. Title 2. Author 3. Fiction

Library of Congress Control Number: 2009941818

ISBN 10: 0615338534
ISBN 13: 978-0-615-33853-8

First, I would like to dedicate this book to my father. His inspiration and guidance in my life, both while he was living and after his passing, showed me the way to lead a good life. Next, my life would not be complete without my loving wife, my wonderful children, my grandchildren, and brothers and sisters. A special thank-you to my daughter for helping me with the computer to complete this work. I love you all and always pray for the best for you. While I was writing this book my family encouraged me to continue and showed me a great deal of patience and understanding.

Finally, thanks to Larry, Olga, Jessica, Jim, and Christina for their help, patience, encouragement, and support. When I first approached them with this book I never thought it would be finished. I owe much gratitude to them for this book finally being printed. Especially thanks to Clyde House for helping me with the computer. Without his help, I never would have been able to complete this.

If this work of love produces fruit, I plan on donating some of the proceeds to various charities that help people starting with Sean Hannity's Freedom Alliance Scholarship Fund. This charity provides scholarships to the children of America's fallen heroes who gave their lives for this country. In these tough economic times I see many hungry people. With that in mind, some of the local food banks may also be receiving aid.

Chapter One

So much of our world is shaped by fate, by kindness and cruelty, by sheer luck, or by things beyond our control. The natural world—plants, trees, and the beautiful blue of the sky or the ragged mountain edge—can seem like a gorgeously wrapped gift, handed over to humanity without any thought or effort, without any work behind it.

But the gifts of nature, like the gifts of God and faith, are so much deeper, and so much more complex, than we could ever imagine. It takes much more than chance for a plant to thrive, to bring forth a shock of deep color in a gentle petal or bright green leaves, all from a miniscule seed. Like the most successful people, a plant, whether it is a flower, a fruit or a tree, must defy the odds, anchor itself against danger, circumstance and neglect, taking advantage of all the good that surrounds it, and use those elements to reach the highest heights.

Of course not all nature, and not all of its plants, is pretty or easy to grow, or handed to us without cost or investment. The delicate, fragile petals of a white pear tree blossom must endure a hundred possible dangers before it brings forth a fat, juicy pear.

Nature itself has an inherent element of what some might describe as simple evil—violent storms, nasty predators, raging fires that torch fertile lands, searing heat that makes life impossible. But like the prettiest flowers or the tallest, strongest trees, a successful life is much more than an accident of nature.

Nature gives us more, much more, than the foods we need to live. On its grandest scale, the Earth gives us an example, a blueprint of life that helps us to know not just how to survive against difficult circumstances or those who would do us harm, but how to overcome those things. The gifts of the earth can show us how to thrive, how to push deep roots into the ground all while battling the forces that would keep us weak or lost, how to protect our vulnerable green leaves from shriveling and crumbling to dust before they can ever reach the sky.

Just as sunshine feeds the flowers and trees, people can take nourishment in the light of God and His love. I have lived my life not only with God but for Him—and like the sun, He has supported me and helped me find my way to a prosperous life.

All of us face pain, harsh conditions and enemies, but no matter where we are born or how we grow up it is our own choices that determine the quality and success of our own lives. Nature can flourish in the countryside just as well as in the concrete canyons of a big city. No matter how closely we are touched by evil, we have the capacity to overcome it. Like the beautiful flower that soaks up all the good around it to produce a stunning bloom, humans must take in the comfort provided by faith, family and hard work to achieve their dreams.

The success of my seventy-two years is not by chance. There is no accident here. Yes, I have always been open to the sustaining light of God's love in my life, and I strive even now to lead a life that honors and obeys the Lord's intentions. And, yes, I was lucky in a way too—lucky to have a strong family, generations of wisdom and experience to draw from, as I established the roots of my character. Each experience of my early years, from the simplest childhood mistakes to the jealously and disdain of those who would do me harm to the gory death brought to our doorstep by World War II—all these things made me who I am.

I have had darkness in my life, times when despair and depression made it feel as if God's love for me was obscured, as if I could no longer take in the warmth of his caring and support. There have been times when I looked at some of those closest to me and saw and felt nothing but threats. But I always listened to my father's words—my father, my hero—who encouraged me to focus on my own work, and not to allow worry, envy, greed or laziness to lead me astray. I learned to look at all that surrounded me, to use the positive forces for my benefit and deflect the negative—and like a beautiful flower, my life has born riches beyond my dreams.

My roots, my early years, were shaped as much by prosperity and love as they were by evil, but far from my current home of America. I had the kind of childhood most only dream of, an ocean away on a small, sun-drenched family farm of fruit trees and vegetables planted among gently rolling green hills. The mountainous spine of central Italy was the backdrop for our tiny town, where everyone seemed to know each other.

Each day my brothers and sisters and I, all eight of us, would perform our chores, caring for the animals, fig and other fruit trees, and picking vegetables on the four or five acres that made up our farm.

It was my father's farm, and his father's land before that. My father, Lorenzo, would work the fields while my mother, Marietta, would sell the food the farm produced. A tiny woman, she would gather up vegetables, figs, pears and other fruits, filling a large basket, lifting the burden high up over her head, and making the mile or so walk into town to sell the produce two or three times a week.

My grandparents were an integral part of life, passing on some of the longest traditions of our family, everything from farming and hunting to the importance of having a sense of humor, faith in God and spirituality. My grandmother would help feed and take care of the children, which was a big task because there were eight of us, while my grandfather took us almost every day to church.

I can't help but smile when thinking of my grandfather, even all these years later. He was a joker, an entertainer. Some of the paths around our town were steep, full of zigzagging trails, and my grandfather would play games on the walk to church. He would sit down, pretending to be tired and needing a rest, urging us to go on without him—then we would come around a bend and he would be there, having taken a shortcut and sprinted ahead. We would come around a curve only to discover him fresh as a daisy.

"What took you so long?" he'd say, grinning at our bewilderment.

It was the late 1930s and while our life was very different then than it is today, it was a good life, a life of peace and plenty. We did not know that it was not going to last, or how much things were going to change.

But even though that time seemed ideal, it wasn't

perfect. Like a young tree buffeted by frost, as a child I had a sense that people did not think much of me. Even though I was one of eight kids, as a child I preferred to play by myself, or to sit quietly and listen to the adults as they talked, instead of always running around with the other children. I usually wouldn't speak up unless I knew what to say. But people often misinterpreted my quiet demeanor and mistakenly believed that I wasn't so smart.

My father, Lorenzo, knew better. He was the star of my life—I trusted everything he said, respected him and adored him as much as any boy could love their father. For a while, my child's mind honestly thought that he and God were one and the same, and I bathed in his love and affection just as a plant does in sunshine. Just after I was born, he had to spend a year in Africa, working for the Italian army. He wasn't away long, but as I grew up I found that one of my favorite places to be was by his side.

One summer day my father was helping out a neighbor, as people often came around for his advice and guidance. My brothers and sisters were running around, playing and chattering, but I, just a young boy, was sitting on the ground nearby, drawing in the dirt and playing with the grass. It probably didn't look like it, but I was listening to all that they talked about.

The men were sipping wine, talking, when the neighbor pointed toward me.

"You've got a nice family, but this little boy," he said. "He looks a little slow."

I'm sure now that the man probably thought I couldn't hear him, or that I wasn't listening or that I didn't understand. He probably never meant to be hurtful. But my father's response is what I remember most.

He took a few steps toward the neighbor and spoke into his ear, but he knew I was listening, and my father talked loudly enough for me to hear.

"This little boy? He's the smartest one of all," my father said.

Hearing those words made me feel so good. All it took was my beloved father's vote of confidence to let me know that it didn't matter what anyone else thought of me.

After that day, I began to bloom, and I realized that the idea that I was dumb, or a little "slow," had always been around, as if it were in the air—but that it wasn't true. I started watching other kids, paying attention to what they did, and more and more I knew that I wasn't dumb at all.

Though I would have almost always rather been by my father's side, the daily grind of work and chores on the farm never stopped. Year-round, there were vegetables to pick, like turnips or broccoli, and we would march out into the slushy snow to collect them. The children would often help by drawing water from the well for the animals or plants. So much of our life came from working the land, which had gentle hills and was at the foot of a mountain about a mile outside the small town of Piglio.

Mother Nature tried to do her best to help us, as fruit trees seemed to spring up from the ground by themselves along with the ones we planted. We grew lots of figs, and pears that were so sweet and so good; I can still taste them today. My mother, Marietta, a woman with just a third-grade education, would load up a basket two or three times a week and walk a mile into town to sell our fruits and vegetables. She spent almost every day working at the market, and always sold a lot of produce and supported the family well.

There were apples, too, which we would store in the attic of our modest home. They were a special type of apple and we could eat them all winter long. There were animals, too, cows and chickens, a pig and a donkey that was more like a pet than anything else.

It was a resourceful lifestyle. My parents even made their own flour from grain, and we would slaughter our own pig to make our bacon and other meats. When we were not on the farm, there was school, sometimes two grades learning in a one-room schoolhouse from the same teacher. Classes were different then than they are today, and we would almost always be in school either in the morning or the afternoon, never all day long.

School was a place of joy for me, another source of

sustenance. I found school to be quite easy and loved it so much, I couldn't wait to go each day. But even though I loved the classroom, the teacher was always shrieking at me. She would yell at me for not paying attention because while she talked, I was usually completing my home work assignments right there in the classroom. For a while, I dreamed I would grow up to be some kind of intellectual and felt that I could never get too far in life without a proper education.

Our home was modest with just a few large rooms, but it was open and airy. Italy has a mild climate and it never gets very cold, not even on the winter nights as the temperatures stayed around the forty-degree mark. While we didn't have any deep freezes it was still cold enough for a fire, and in the wintertime it was my grandfather's job to mind the kitchen hearth. I would often sit near him, keeping warm and sometimes roasting chestnuts. On the winter evenings, my grandfather would tend to the fire, and the adults would gather and pray the rosary. Often we had a cauldron hanging on a chain over the flames, to cook in. My family used to cook delicious meals, the scent of boiling chestnuts filling the air; we used everything that farm could produce.

The farm was originally my grandfather's land. But it was a rough time to be a farmer and in the early 1900s, he often had to patrol the property to protect his produce. A longtime hunter, grandfather used to brag that he was such a good shot, he could take aim at a fox all the way over on another hill and nail it with his shotgun. In those days, though, he had bigger things than pesky foxes to worry about.

At that time, everyone was really on their own—if he wanted to guard his land and his livelihood, he had to do it himself, and most of the time it was his own neighbors that he had to guard against.

Grandfather would make rounds each night with a shotgun, like a soldier guarding a citadel. He'd walk through the dark by himself, giving off a blast now and then from afar to scare the thieves, but the sound of the shotgun never really kept the irritating bandits away for good and he never shot at anyone because he never really wanted to hurt anybody.

One night, on his lonely patrol, grandfather came upon the familiar sounds of just such a thief but chose not to use his shotgun. Instead, he decided to have some fun. As he walked he heard a voice in the dark, full of frustration, and he heard noise; it turned out to be a neighbor trying to steal bundles of wheat straight from the field.

My grandfather slowed down, creeping silently and unseen behind some brush to watch the man, Ernesto, struggle to gather up the valuable bundles. In the dark and by himself, Ernesto was having trouble and, thinking he was alone, began to loudly curse the name of God as he tried to take what wasn't his.

But instead of throwing off a blast from his shotgun to scare Ernesto away, my grandfather had another idea.

Struggling and cursing, wrapped up in his illicit task, Ernesto probably never even heard my grandfather walking nearby.

Suddenly, a deep, booming voice echoed in the black night:

"Eh, what is this Ernesto? What are you doing? What are you saying, taking my name in vain?"

Ernesto jumped, scared out of his skin by the voice of "God" and leaping high into the air, screaming at the top of his lungs. He dropped that bundle of wheat so fast, it might as well have been on fire. In a flash the would-be thief ran like hell, sprinting out of there faster than lightning—all without a single blast from my grandfather's shotgun. And as the frightened man bolted out of sight, my mischievous grandfather emerged from his hiding spot, bursting out laughing at his own gag, getting a good kick out of the sight of his shaken neighbor who had been shamed and scared by "God."

My grandfather was the joker; he always kept things light. My father, on the other hand, was the one none of us could stand to disappoint. He ruled our home not with cold cruelty or an iron will but with a powerful warmth and positive influence that commanded respect and obedience.

Our kitchen fire, like in most Italian homes, was burning almost all the time. You needed a fire for pretty much everything back then—boiling the water and cooking food. The fireplace, with the cauldron hanging above, was always set up and ready to go because the fire was needed so often. The pieces of brush and wood were usually nearby, as were the matches.

I knew where the matches were, and one summer day when I was four years old I snuck over to the fireplace like a sly little imp, snatched the matches and flew out of the kitchen.

I didn't make a clean escape, however. My grandmother, she was always in the kitchen, and she saw what I had done and gave chase.

You have to remember that we lived on a farm, and because of the animals we always had hay and straw around. It was dangerous for a little kid to be running around with matches! My grandmother said:

"What do you have in your hand?"

"Nothing," I called out, trying to sound innocent.

I made it all the way outside, running as fast as my little legs could carry me, but she followed after me and managed to catch me, grabbing the matches out of my chubby little hands.

I don't even remember now why I wanted the matches or what I was going to do with them. But getting caught suddenly made me so mad, anger boiled up inside of my little body. I yelled at my grandmother, using an Italian expression that basically meant that I hoped she would get hit by lightning. I don't think I even understood what I was really saying; I was just repeating an expression I had heard. What can I say—I guess it was a rough country back then!

My grandmother heard what I said but didn't react. Instead of becoming angry or yelling at me, she stopped. She just looked at me, thinking.

Then she sat me down and said:

"Is that how you talk to me?"

She paused for a moment, deliberating, and then made her decision.

"When he gets home, I'm going to tell your father what you said."

My tiny world stopped, and immediately I was paralyzed with fear. It was the worst thing my grandmother could have said, and I felt like I was going to die. My father was everything to me—my mentor, my idol, my God. I loved him so much, at that age I thought he was without sin himself.

I didn't want him to know what I had done. I spent the long hours that afternoon furtively hoping and praying he wouldn't find out, hoping that somehow my grandmother would forget to tell him or change her mind.

But she did not. When my father got home she told him what I had done right away. He turned to me and asked me in a stern voice if it was true.

Frozen in place, I could only nod my head.

"I cannot hear you," my father said, standing over me.

"Yes," I managed to squeak out.

I couldn't even look at him.

He asked me why I'd done it, and I told him I didn't know why.

"Don't you know that what you said and did is bad?" he asked, but I was so upset I couldn't even answer him.

"Would you do it again?" he said.

I quickly told him that no, I would not.

I really thought I had done something terrible, and it was one of the worst feelings of my life. I was so sorry, and even though he knew that I was regretful my father wanted to make sure I understood, and he sent me to bed without supper.

Now that I am a father and grandfather myself, I know it must have been tough for him to send a little four-year-old boy to bed with no food for the night, but my father always wanted us to understand when we had done something wrong and he wanted to make sure we wouldn't do it again. I went up to my room and couldn't stop thinking about what I had done.

Later in the evening my father went outside for a little while, and my mother snuck up the stairs to my room with a plate of food.

"Eat fast, your father's not here right now," she said.

I knew my mother had good intentions, and that she felt sorry for me, but I couldn't eat. I told my mother no and pushed the food away because I was so upset with myself.

I was so upset, but more with myself for doing something wrong than with my father for punishing me. Somebody else might have been angry because they got sent to bed without supper, but I knew I had made a big mistake, and my father had every right to punish me. It was a testing of the strength of my character, and it helped me realize what I was made of and how strong I was.

And even though it felt so terrible at the time, I now feel that taking those matches, getting caught and being punished was a good thing. Like a sapling whose roots are digging deep into the earth, learning from that mistake helped my character take root. I knew, in my heart and soul, how wrong it was to steal, and I took my father's punishment as encouragement to do the right thing, which only helped me grow and mature.

My father's sense of character, his strength, was something, it seemed, he'd always had. I remember hearing the stories of when he was younger and serving in the army, how even though he had a limited education he was able to share important lessons with almost everyone he met and make good friends along the way.

When my father was growing up, it was common for people in Italy to have a limited education. He only made it through the fifth grade, but when he was in the army he attained the rank of corporal.

When my father joined the army, he worked in the communications office and showed many talents, including math and the ability to do a little calligraphy. He was also a skilled barber, with all the tools and equipment he needed to do a proper job. He was not only our family barber but it was a task he performed while in the army, in the days when he himself had hair that was a bit long.

It was a look that one of his captains didn't take a liking to, but my father was sort of a joker in those days. When the captain came over and asked him to go see the barber, my father said, "OK." Then he tried to play stupid and visited the barber—without getting a haircut.

One time he was left in charge of a group of guys and had them doing chores such as sweeping and taking the garbage out. Everyone was on a schedule and knew which tasks they had to perform, but there was one soldier who just didn't show up.

As it turned out, that soldier was the son of someone either very rich or very important—the difference didn't much matter. While the soldier was a nice guy, no one demanded much of him because of his family connections. He got an easier time of it than most of the other guys because everybody knew who he was.

But my father did not play that kind of game. He believed that people should be treated equally, and it was a philosophy he lived by. That day, my father pretended not to know about the soldier's status and had him listed on the schedule of chores anyway. In fact, my father had stuck the guy with the worst chore of them all: picking up the horse poop!

Well, that soldier was so unaccustomed to work, and to anyone asking him to work, that he never even looked on that schedule. He figured no one would bother him, and on the day the chores were supposed to be done, the soldier was not there.

So my father sent someone out to look for him, which was virtually unheard of. The soldier apologized, but he was also a bit surprised.

"I'm sorry, but don't you know who I am?" the soldier asked.

My father maintained his charade.

"Who are you?" he asked innocently.

The soldier seemed stunned again, but my father didn't keep the ploy going for much longer. He told the soldier he would help him with the work, and they completed the task together. In the end, they became good friends and went for beers together almost every day. The soldier even took my father to dinner at his family's mansion.

But that's the way my father was. He didn't treat people differently because of how much money they had or who they knew. He didn't see people that way. He got along with everyone and always just focused on the task before him with an attention that sustained him and gave him the strength to get through whatever came his way.

So by the time he had me and I was old enough to steal the matches from the kitchen, my father had a long history of doing the right thing and encouraging that in others.

Not long after that incident with the matches, my grandmother became sick and was in bed for months. Those days are blurred together in my mind, and I do not remember much about her because I was so young. I still have a picture of her from when she was feeding me as a youngster. I do recall that when my younger brother was born, she started taking care of him more instead of me, and that made me jealous. Her long illness took its toll, and she finally succumbed, dying just before my fifth birthday.

My grandmother's death ushered in a new phase of our lives, though we didn't realize it then. We were about to enter a period of storminess that threatened our very existence, and the peace and prosperity of our bountiful life was about to be battered by world politics and gruesome violence. My father and grandfather had always trusted in God, and felt that the Lord would take care of us as long as we lived a life that honored him.

I can remember a day when a group of people came marching down the main road just outside our home. They were shouting, “The war is over—long live our peace!” It was around the time of Benito Mussolini’s surrender. But in actuality it was just the beginning, for this curious moment presaged the German troops’ moving into Italy. Little did we know how much life was about to change, and how lucky we were to have God by our sides as World War II swept the Italian countryside.

Chapter Two

I don't remember exactly when World War II started, or the beginning of it in our lives. Like the gathering of dark clouds on the horizon, the war swirled around us for months as the fighting crept closer to Piglio, first with the battles in northern Africa and then the invasion of Sicily. As the Allied forces took over southern Italy and crept northward in their battle against Adolf Hitler, the presence of the German soldiers quickly increased around us and eventually the brutality of war was literally outside our door.

Once the fighting began it seemed like the war had been going on forever, instantly. I was just seven years old. It seemed at times as if the light of God's love was blocked from our lives, but His guiding hand found a way to reach and sustain us even in the worst moments.

Our peaceful, sleepy farm existence became fraught with danger as German soldiers and fascists turned our world upside down. The lush, green countryside and family farms became casualties as much as our friends and neighbors did, and the picturesque landscape became the unlikely backdrop for countless dogfights—the sights, sounds and smells of which I can never forget.

My father found himself constantly negotiating dangerous elements including starvation, violent, callous German soldiers and the desperation and need of our neighbors and friends, all while steering clear of the conflict that was raging around us. He did whatever he could to provide for his brood, braving the dark nights just so we would be well-fed during more than a year of intense conflict.

Once the war came, there was no more of the school I loved so much. I can't remember if I ever even started the third grade in the tiny, one-room schoolhouse. Young men and teenage boys, including my older brother, were forced to hide from the Germans for fear of being taken by the soldiers to work in Germany, or to fight.

It was a scary time. At first my brother, who was sixteen, would flee any time German soldiers were around, cowering in the attic where we kept our winter apples. But it became clear that hiding in the attic was no solution. What if the soldiers had asked us where he was and we lied, only to have them discover him in the house? It would have been no good and was only a recipe for big trouble. The best thing to do was to get him out of there and he, like many others, fled into the nearby mountains. We didn't see him much during that time but he wasn't far away, and we would hear news of him through the grapevine of refugees that soon developed.

Those refugees lived in hiding and fear of being taken. They lived by surviving off the land and the generosity of local families whenever possible.

The soldiers, armed to the teeth, were a formidable presence, and just as the war closed in on us around November 1943, they were everywhere. Often the soldiers were German and were difficult to communicate with because most of them didn't speak Italian.

Sometimes abusive and violent, the soldiers would take whatever they wanted, usually food, and they would force their way into people's homes just so they would have a place to sleep. If you crossed the soldiers or angered them in any way, there was always the chance they could shoot you down. Even though this wasn't our war, we and all the other people caught in the middle feared for our lives and had to be careful of everything we said and did.

As the war dragged on, it was like an action movie unfolding in and around our tiny farm. We could always hear the air battles before we saw the military planes themselves, the *rat-a-tat-tat* sound of their artillery heralding the arrival of battle. The Americans planes were always in formation, with no less than twelve planes traveling together at once.

The air encounters often ended with the fighters abandoning their crafts. We watched many pilots and soldiers parachute out of their planes, floating to the ground.

There were seas of soldiers moving through our town. Often, the Germans would march along the road outside our house under the cover of night; the only thing visible was the tiny, red glow of their cigarettes.

The most heated and intense conflicts were just about twenty miles west of Piglio, in the town of Cassino, which became a major battleground. Tens of thousands of American and German soldiers were killed in the fighting there, and the town was bombed mercilessly as it served as a critical flashpoint in the tug of war between the Allied forces and Germany.

The war became so intense, the air at times seemed full of bullets and bomb fragments, and there was so much artillery my father and grandfather had to teach us how to dive into a trench or a ditch to protect ourselves the second we heard any gunfire. My grandfather, who always tried to keep things light, used to joke that we had to make sure to protect ourselves, because if we ever got hit in the head with a metal fragment from a bomb or artillery, we wouldn't be able to understand things anymore. With death so constantly close at hand, I guess it was better to teach us with a joke than fear.

It must have been so hard for my grandfather to joke around during those years. My grandmother had only recently died after a long illness, and he was watching the lands that he and his relatives before him had held for years be ruined by months of fighting, artillery and fire.

Then my uncle became the victim of German soldiers, who honored a barbaric rule of invasion that mandated that for each German soldier killed, ten Italian lives would be taken in exchange. We never really knew why my uncle was chosen for such a cruel end. There was a rumor that he had a machine gun and he may have been rounded up in such a group of ten because of that—or simply because he angered the Germans in some way. He was shot to death by a firing squad during the war, and we were powerless to do anything to stop it. The cold reality was there wasn't much we could do.

My grandfather himself had his own brush with death when he was taken by a group of German soldiers. These soldiers may as well have been terrorists. They stalked the town, grabbing people at random from their homes and families and holding them against their will for days.

Captive, the people didn't know what to think

or what to do. There seemed to be no escape and the soldiers only added to the suffering, teasing and tormenting their victims without mercy.

"Get ready to meet your maker," they would say to their trembling victims, cigarettes hanging from their mouths. "Make peace with your God."

Snatching a shaken man from the group, the soldiers would push the person out in front of them, forcing them to take what were probably the most harrowing steps of their lives and threatening them all the while, their guns raised and at the ready.

Then, as the end seemed inevitable and the victims tried to prepare for the unthinkable, the sound they heard was the soldiers, who would only mimic the sound of gunfire, laughing loudly at their own cruel joke and the relief of the abused and frightened people.

It was pure evil at work only for the amusement of the torturers. We had no idea what had happened, knowing only that my grandfather was missing for a few days. The whole episode was strange, because soldiers didn't normally target older adults.

Thankfully, somehow, my grandfather was released a few days later and made his way home to us physically unharmed.

With this cruelty so present in our lives, it might be hard to imagine that the war was not all bad. There were dozens of little miracles through the worst of the fighting, as if God were showing us that He was still there, by our side, through all the death and destruction.

While my father, just like everyone else, wanted the war to end, he had been a soldier himself at one time and he never took offense with the soldiers, and even in all that chaos tried to treat everyone fairly and nicely. He did his best to communicate with the Germans and even though to some it was unthinkable, my father always tried to show respect.

And not all the soldiers were so sadistic. Those who could speak a little Italian almost always talked about how much they hated Hitler, and how they wished the war would end so they could return home.

One evening, there was a small group of five or six soldiers walking by our home. They turned out to be English troops trying to make an escape after their plane had been shot down in one of the battles. My father brought them into the house and fed them, sharing very good wine because he recognized that they were friends who were working with the Americans to try to liberate us. He knew they needed help to avoid capture, so my father brought them up into the mountains near Piglio, showing them a cave to hide in.

Every couple of days for about a month he would regularly return to that cave, bringing the Englishmen food and water. But one day, the soldiers weren't there. We don't know if they were discovered and taken by the Germans or if they simply moved on.

Even though he had served in the Italian army, when World War II came around my father's loyalties were with one group: his family. He always said it wasn't his war, that his main concern was caring for his family. And while many of the Germans were inhumane, not all were like that, and no matter what, my father always treated the German soldiers like friends—he knew he wasn't going to be able to influence them in any way, and because he was so kind to them, they were often respectful of him and his responsibility to his family.

As I'm older now with my own family, I realize how smart my father's strategy for dealing with the Germans was. There were so many things happening beyond his control, but my father focused on what he could control and succeeded, with the help of God, in getting us through those difficult times as unscathed as possible.

He took that responsibility seriously. Each week, my father would load up a cart with precious supplies like wine and olive oil, doing his best to conceal what he had inside. At night, he would brave the dark, full of its marching German soldiers, and make the dangerous, nighttime trips down through the valley to meet with other farmers, with his only company along the way being the family donkey.

It was a treacherous journey through areas full of fascists who were working with the Germans, and sometimes he had to hide out of sight for fear of raising the attention of passing soldiers. Despite the risks, the trip was worth it as he would trade his supplies with other farmers there, getting flour, beans and wheat in exchange for his wine and oil.

It's not that my father or his clandestine trips went unnoticed. Along the way the fascists would stop my father and question him, but somehow he always managed to avoid having the valuable goods taken and was able to talk his way out of any encounter. Even in those dark times, people were sympathetic when he talked about how he never bothered anyone and had to feed his six or seven children at home. My father felt that God was with him, protecting him and us on those trips, which helped us survive.

Because of my father's night journeys, our family had more than enough food even as neighbors went hungry and the refugees in the nearby mountains starved. But my father knew goodwill and a kind word wouldn't be enough to truly protect us, and under the cover of night he hid the extra foodstuffs in many places. We had food hidden everywhere, including in a barrel in the ground of a small, straw hut on our farm. The barrel wasn't airtight but it sufficed, and he disguised the floor by using straw and hay to cover it up.

One day a group of German soldiers appeared. The captain was brusque and seemed preoccupied. My father could only stand by and watch as the German captain barked orders at his soldiers to put the group's horses out of sight in that straw hut. We didn't know why they wanted to hide or what they were so frantic about. They were in a hurry, angry and appeared to be distracted.

But my father knew he had to do something because having the horses in that hut meant our supplies were at risk. He tried over and over again to get the captain's attention, but his efforts were in vain as the man just brushed him off and continued to order his troops around. Getting more and more worried, my agitated, frantic father moved down the line, trying to talk to each of the soldiers and get the attention of anyone who would listen to him before finally finding a soldier who spoke Italian.

"Listen, if you want to take the stuff in there, then take it," my father told the soldier. "Just leave a little for me. But if one of those horses pees in there it's all ruined."

At last, the message got through. The soldier got the captain's attention and told him what my father had been trying to say. You would have expected the Germans to react greedily, taking all the foodstuffs for themselves. But that's not what happened.

Suddenly there was a lot of yelling and waving among the soldiers, but we didn't understand at first what was going on. Then they got the horses out of that straw hut. Just as harried as they'd come in, the captain moved his soldiers along, never touching the food and wine that we kept in secret and never returning to raid the treasure either.

We kept the secret of our survival close, but always shared what we had with neighbors and the refugees, who were hungry and didn't have their own resources.

Refugees would often come out of the mountains looking for sustenance and my mother, who was pregnant by then, always did her best to feed them. We still had chickens and cows, which meant that we had valuable milk and eggs, and some ladies would come to our home because they knew my mother would share milk with them for their babies.

She always had corn bread cooking in the oven, and outside, in a large, metal pan sixteen inches wide and about a foot high, that she set over a fire, my mother would make beans and lentils, cooking them through. There were never any leftovers.

One day, a man about six feet tall showed up. He seemed at once both robust and hungry and approached my mother, asking to be fed. My mother asked him to wait just a few minutes.

Rushing inside, my mother filled an aluminum container with the cooked beans and a piece of corn bread.

But as she emerged from thc house, the hungry man was shamed by what he saw. The sight of that tiny, pregnant woman walking like a pied piper, surrounded by half a dozen children of her own to feed gave the man pause. Quickly he changed his mind and he tried to refuse the food he had just been begging for.

Arguing with him, my mother wouldn't hear of it. But the man insisted.

"I'm not going to take food from these kids," the man admitted, a stoic look on his face as he shook his head.

Like so many, he had no idea about all the extra food my parents had stored up.

My mother had to plead with him to take the food, finally convincing him to eat.

"God will provide for my children," she insisted.

Finally, his hunger got the better of him and the man relented, taking the container. He sat and gobbled that food down so fast he almost choked himself. But as he finished and lifted his head from the plate he was again confronted by the scene of this woman and her youngsters clamoring around. He couldn't take it. The man seemed overcome with guilt and when he got up to leave my mother had to plead with him to take some extra food along.

She gave him some dried figs and chestnuts, and he reluctantly accepted the offering, proclaiming that it would last him a few weeks.

"God bless you," he said, kissing my mother's hand as he left. He walked off into the mountains from which he had come. We didn't see him again.

It wasn't the only time that the image of my mother

with all those children also affected those around us. Even the Germans took pity and tried to help.

One day a pair of Germans came to our house, searching it from top to bottom. We don't even know what they were looking for, though most likely they were trying to find food. It was a younger soldier and an older one and they looked everywhere, in every cabinet and cubby, and opened everything, turning our house upside down in the process.

The older German soldier found a jug that we had filled with sausage and oil, but the jug was high up and when the soldier tipped it over to look inside, he spilled a bit on his shirt. Everyone froze because even though it was a funny moment, we couldn't laugh. You never knew whether you were dealing with friendly Germans or not and if they were in the mood to and took any offense, they could have just shot us. The soldiers took a few things and then left.

But a few days later, at night, we heard someone on the back steps. Looking outside, we saw one of the soldiers who had searched our house. It was the younger German returning, and he was hauling a 100-pound bag of flour over his shoulder, a special commodity in those days.

The sack was marked with the stamp of the German army. That soldier was so strong and even though he couldn't speak any Italian it was clear that he had taken the supplies from himself and his colleagues to try to help my family, taking a great risk that the loss of the flour would be discovered and he would be punished. But he saw my mother with all those children around and he felt bad for us, not knowing that we had provisions hidden all over the place. We emptied the flour, and the soldier took the sack back so that his deception wouldn't be discovered. He never returned.

Not all the soldiers were cruel. There was one soldier who showed off pictures of a young child back home—his child, whom he hadn't even been able to meet. That soldier may have been an "enemy," but he was nice to us and took a liking to my younger sister, who was just a toddler back then and about the same age as the soldier's child. In her, he saw the child he had been missing so badly.

Sometimes language barriers caused trouble all on their own. Soldiers never forced their way into my family's home to sleep, but one night they came close, and our family's inability to communicate with them almost prompted a shooting. A pair of German soldiers came by with the request and my father waved his arms, indicating that they should go ahead, before he went back inside the house.

It was around Christmastime. My father had been getting ready to slaughter a pig. He had all the equipment he needed laid out and ready to go, but for a stranger it must have been a gruesome scene: large, sharp knives lying around and a big, twenty-four-inch-high cauldron all set out and ready for the job, which was to begin the next morning.

For us, there was nothing odd about it. Slaughtering the pig ourselves was important; it allowed us to have our own meat and things like bacon and prosciutto.

Even though my father told the German soldiers that they should go ahead and spend the night if they wished, they looked around and immediately began to wonder what was going on. My father went inside, not knowing that the German soldiers had begun to feel that with all the knives around, maybe something wasn't quite right at this house they had come to.

The soldiers, who didn't speak Italian, began badgering my father with questions, pointing to the knives. Maybe they wondered if they had stumbled upon some sort of murderer or criminal and couldn't leave until they investigated.

Finally, he realized what was upsetting them. They probably thought they were going to be murdered in their sleep! He tried to explain but they couldn't understand him, and wouldn't walk away.

My father frantically tried to figure out how to tell them he was simply getting ready for slaughtering a pig, but nothing seemed to work and the soldiers were only getting more anxious. It wasn't until my father finally was able to find a picture of a pig in a textbook.

He pointed to the picture and then at the knives, and somehow motioned what his plans were until eventually, they seemed to understand—and quickly began to laugh. The stress and nervous tension that had been building was quickly relieved, the soldiers and my father dissolving into laughter. Then they became something more than soldiers on an angry mission. They became friends.

But the German army, like any large group, included a wide variety of personalities and our inability to communicate with some of them made for weird situations. One time a beautiful lady with a young child came to our home, asking my mother for milk for the baby.

That day, there was a German soldier around our house. He was nice at first, but he had found a flask of wine and grabbed it, gulping it down. Maybe he just got too drunk, because he suddenly started to chase the woman around our property. At one point, he had a sickle in his hands as he pursued her; maybe the soldier meant it as a joke but it was a terrifying sight and the woman was so scared she didn't know what to do. The soldier either didn't understand or didn't care what he was doing to the woman.

When my mother saw what was going on she tried to stop the soldier, even though she herself was very pregnant.

The soldier disregarded my mother's attempts

to stop him until finally she jumped on his back and pounded him with her fists. Finally, she was able to tell him that she was going to go find his captain.

That made the soldier stop, and he dropped the sharp sickle. His face changed, and it was easy to see that he was now scared too, and after what seemed like an eternity he left.

Another time, a pair of soldiers sat down to Easter dinner with my family.

We may not have wanted that kind of company, but we couldn't ever refuse or be rude when the soldiers wanted something, no matter how much we might have wanted to. They took a disliking to our dog that was chained up outside and barking at them; they threatened to shoot the animal if it didn't stop. My mother had created a nice dinner with egg fettuccine, brown, roasted lamb and red homemade wine. One of the soldiers, who was too young to even be a lieutenant, said, "I never had a good meal like that!" But when my mother cooked, everybody said that!

The dangers of the war could never be forgotten, though, no matter how many soldiers we became friendly with. One night, a captain in the German army was killed, and though many people died during the conflict, this time was different. Though the captain's wife was a civilian, she traveled from Germany when she learned of her husband's death. When she arrived, somehow the distraught wife was able to convince the soldiers to take drastic action—they set fire to all the lands around, torching anything that would burn.

Bright flames sparked up all around the countryside, and my family watched the burning flames as they crept along, making their slow, insatiable approach toward our house and farm. My father estimated that the blaze would reach us by five or six a.m., and we knew that we would have to evacuate. But just about a mile from our home, the fire stopped. We never had to evacuate and while we didn't learn the real reason why the flames were doused, we believed that the soldiers were ordered to find those who had actually killed that German captain.

For a time the bombardment of nearby Cassino meant that large-scale attacks were unfolding closer to our farm than ever, putting on a show that was at once spectacular and stunning.

There is one dogfight I'll never forget, between four or five small, German planes and an American contingent of fighter planes, which showed the determination of the Allied forces. The Americans, who always flew in formations of twelve or more planes, were on their way to bomb Cassino, a crucial battleground in the Allied strategy of winning ground back from the Germans.

We could hear the exchange of gunfire before the planes came into sight. While that fight was anything but an even match, the smaller, German planes were able to break up the dozen American planes flying in formation. Two of the American craft took fire from the Germans, sustaining serious damage.

The Germans were fighting like hell and while the rest of the American contingent flew on to Cassino, smoke began pouring from their crippled counterparts, and they quickly started to lose altitude. The crews inside were forced to eject and suddenly the sky was dotted with men, four or five from each plane floating to Earth as their parachutes opened above them.

As the American soldiers landed on the ground their planes ran straight into the mountainside, exploding into balls of flame.

Then, out of nowhere, fifteen American fighter planes zipped through the sky, coming so fast the air whistled as they moved. It was a massive response that scattered what remained of the Germans, who dove out of sight of the Americans, who used machine guns to cut down any of the enemy they could see.

The American support contingent split up, with four or five of the planes sent to escort the original group of twelve on their mission to Cassino while others stayed behind, circling in the heavens to guard the Americans who had been forced to parachute out of their planes. The other fighters were sent to pursue the Germans and finish the fight. The sight of those planes diving toward each other and twisting in the air, along with the sounds of those fighters exchanging gunfire in the skies above our heads, was, in a way, so much better than any action movie I have ever seen.

But sometimes, the movie became too real. There was a beautiful spring night, a lovely May evening, and I remember so clearly the American military planes racing across the sky.

They dropped special lights on parachutes that, as they fell, lit up the whole area as if it were daylight. But the effect was hardly that of the sun. The light gave the Americans a clear sight of the German soldiers they were targeting, so there wouldn't be any mistakes.

The Americans were dropping massive, painfully precise bombs that destroyed not just their enemies but everything around as well. Somehow there were no innocent casualties, even though the bombs landed only 150 yards from our home and our neighbors.

The explosives decimated the area, devastating the once-bountiful land along with everything around. The annihilation came so close it included my neighbor's property. The whole episode took about forty-five minutes.

In less than an hour, the American attack had left dead soldiers littering the ground like bloodied, smoldering leaves. But things were so bad for those living in the shadow of the war that there could be no respect for the dead. Once the bombing stopped, people in the area came out of hiding like rats scurrying to devour bits of uneaten food left behind.

The people were so desperate for anything of value that they began raiding the soldiers' bodies, stripping them down and stealing for themselves anything that might be useful, such as their boots or belts.

Several hours later, some authority, the local police or someone, came around. They chased the looters off but showed no more respect for the remains than anyone else. One by one, the authorities would collect the dead, dragging the bloody, broken bodies to the side of the road. Eventually they had a mound of dead bodies three or four feet deep, and five or six feet wide.

There was no funeral, no memorial, no honor or ceremony for those who had been killed. There was nowhere to take the remains away to. The authorities simply set fire to the pile and left it there, smoldering and stinking, for the residents to live with.

The pile of dead bodies burned and smoked for days, smelling awful. The stench was unavoidable; the burning left an acrid odor that hung in the air. But the ghastly result of the bombing didn't stop there. With no resources of its own, the authority handed out brown bags to the people. They asked them to perform the grisly task of scouring the ground, collecting evidence of the attack and evidence of the death—including pieces of flesh—and bringing it to the blaze they had started.

My mother tried to keep us away as best she could but it was tough when the battle was so close at hand.

She stopped me before I had much of a chance to become too steeped in the dangerous, disgusting and disgraceful work.

The pile of bodies brought tears to my mother's eyes, the very sight of it causing her to lament. She would remark out loud about the dead soldiers' poor mothers and wonder how they could endure such losses, or if they would ever even know what had happened.

But even when my mother tried to keep me from it, to shield me from the macabre, I couldn't stay away. I would sneak back to the window and watch or slip outside and be close to it. It left an indelible print on my mind. For years the scenes I took in that day were etched in my brain and refused to leave, and would replay in my mind over and over again like a film that I couldn't turn off or get away from. It was no longer entertainment to have fighter planes engage in combat over our heads.

I would lay in my bed at night and in my mind would watch the American planes flying overhead and see the bombing play out again and again. The dead bodies, the burning pile—these images plagued my mind and imagination for years.

But the horrific scenes actually heralded the end of the war, which came in waves over the Italian countryside in the weeks just shy of my eighth birthday.

Miraculously, it was easy for most of the farmers to reclaim the land and get back the life they'd had before the war, though the site that had been bombed by the Americans showed how bad things could have been.

The accuracy of the American bombardment was startling, and though it was only about 150 yards from our house, our property was virtually untouched while the area that was hit was ruined. Apples, pear trees, all the plants were ruined. It took five years for them to bear fruit again.

Even though the bombing had targeted the property next to ours, only about five percent of our farm sustained serious damage. My parents were able to continue farming as they had before, and the production of fruits and vegetables for my mother to sell did not change.

Though the war was ending, what it left behind was a landscape littered with damage, metal fragments and unexploded ordinances. People were trying to do whatever they could make money.

Some of the only work available was to gather up the metal, which was now ubiquitous, including the bullets, fragments of bombs and large rifle shells. It was more dangerous than anyone knew at the time but the metal was valuable and could fetch good prices.

Even though I was so small, not even ten years old, I was picking up as much metal as I could, like everyone else. We scoured the land carefully, using metal stakes. We would punch at the ground, digging and moving the dirt away to reveal the precious materials.

The practice was quickly stopped because there were so many live explosives, like cannon shells of all sizes, left in the ground. Many people were injured when they used their crude tools and accidentally unleashed the explosives. Such things were unforgiving and once they were struck almost always gave way, giving off loud, scary sounds and pulverizing blasts. The lucky ones wouldn't be killed by them. The fortunate people were only maimed, losing eyes, limbs or their arms or legs. Once in a while we'd hear a sudden explosion as the ordnances were struck, and the victims were all around.

Nobody realized that once the war ended the danger of death and mutilation would continue to be so close. Finally the authorities went around to all the houses, warning people to stop collecting the metal and teaching them that they shouldn't touch anything like that.

For those who had lost loved ones in the war, recovery must have felt like an impossibility. My family was so fortunate, and life began to recapture its peaceful flow in fairly short order—though the coming years would bring us changes we couldn't have imagined.

One of the blessings of that time was that almost immediately, school began again and for a few months we were able to get a sense of normalcy. I had a few months of third grade, but the year was cut short as the area struggled to replace its infrastructure and the people just tried to get by. We spent that summer just working to recover what we had, and in the fall I went to fourth grade as I normally would have.

I was able to go to school for the next couple of years, through the fifth grade, but then there were no more classes in our town. I desperately wanted to continue my education, to keep going to school. I not only loved class but, even though I was just twelve years old, I knew how important an education was to my future and felt lost knowing that I would not be able to go.

But going to school seemed impossible. There were no classes beyond the fifth grade in our town. And though there was a school about fifteen miles away, the war had so annihilated the transportation systems and roads that fifteen miles seemed an insurmountable distance, one which we children were too young to navigate by ourselves.

Life was changing in other ways as well, because it was around that time that my brave, focused father, who had been able to do anything and always protected us, became sick. It was the beginning of a long illness that changed him from a vibrant man to one who was always in pain and unable to walk.

If my father had been well, there would have been no question—we would have found a way to get to school. But he wasn't well, and life shifted.

I tried to talk to him once about school but he was in such pain that I could not bring myself to force the issue, and I let it go. Our once peaceful, prosperous life had become a bad situation.

When there was no more school my life was vastly different. Though the war was horrible, it taught me to pay attention to my surroundings, to listen more than to speak, and how treating people fairly is, in the end, the best way to be, even when those people are evil or abusive. Without the war, I might not have become the man I am.

But at that time, with my father taken from me by illness and being robbed of school, I felt like I was adrift at sea. I would continue to work on the farm, doing chores and feeding the cows but that is not a life, nor the makings of a future. I didn't know what to do with myself and the big family joke was that I was lazy. They always used to say that my favorite thing to do was eat, and that my favorite place to be was the dinner table. And, cruelly, people talked as if I would never amount to anything, never grow up and get a good job or make any money.

Eventually, we would move away from Piglio, where my family had lived for so long and been so successful, to a different town in Italy a little closer to Rome. We didn't move far away, but the suddenly bad parts of life didn't change much.

Without an education, I feared that all the negative talk about me might turn out to be true. I knew I wasn't dumb or lazy, but also I knew that one couldn't get far in the world, even in the 1940s, without school. I didn't know what to do or where to turn.

Chapter Three

World War II was a brutal time and in many ways, it was unnatural to live for so long with such violence and stress. But nature, like God, is not only about what is pretty or easy or untroubled. Some of the most severe violence—hurricanes, earthquakes, volcanic eruptions—is created by Mother Nature herself. Yet after the difficult events, life blooms anew or is revived.

Like the sunlight, God's love is not meant to shield us from pain. Obeying the will of God does not give us a free pass in life. Rather, putting your faith in God is like having a guiding force on your side, one that helps in dire moments but does not control. A force that supports and sustains if you let it.

Just as nothing stops the sunlight, nothing can truly

obscure God's love for us, and we could feel His presence in our lives many times during the war. Though my family was not completely spared, we were very lucky. And while life was forever changed, things slowly returned to normal in the days and months immediately following World War II, as if my childhood had been on pause and was now moving forward again.

When my extended family would get together they'd talk about the war and the damage it had wrought, usually blaming Mussolini for it. They would lament along with their gossip and chatter, and even though I was usually the quiet one, sometimes I couldn't help myself as I listened to the adults.

"Many people have lost somebody, but we are all alive," I'd say, popping up from a corner where I had been listening, and making them laugh as I offered my hopeful commentary.

Just as I watched everything during the war, I found that observing the adults around me and their conversations taught me much. While my mother would shoo away my older siblings, I was like a little fox hidden in plain sight, absorbing everything I heard.

In a way, it was insulting. They ignored me because they did not think much of me, and that's the way it seemed to always be for me. I never reacted or spoke out or made a scene, so people figured I didn't understand.

I was learning a lot about life though. Neighbors

and relatives would come to my house and gossip, and once, my cousin even began talking nastily about my mother behind her back.

She talked on before her mother, my aunt, realized I was there. My aunt kicked her daughter under the table like a reflex, telling the girl to shut up and glancing at me apprehensively because she saw the look on my face and my raised eyebrows when I heard them saying nasty things about my mother. But really, no one was too worried. They just assumed that I didn't really understand, though nothing was further from the truth. In the end, people would talk like I wasn't there at all.

The war brought death so close for so long you'd think we had developed some immunity from danger and fear, but one of the riskiest episodes of my life actually happened after the Germans left, at our home in Piglio.

Our home was modest but comfortable, and because we were on a farm, the life and business of that became intertwined with our living space—such as the attic we used to store winter apples. My father had built a space attached to the side of the house, a sort of shelter for the bales of hay and bundles of straw and brush we used to make our cooking fires.

I was around eight or nine years old when one day I noticed a space between the bales of straw and the wall of the shelter. The opening was in a bottom corner, near the door, and turned out to be a long hole that went on for about eight feet and would have been too tough for an adult to get into.

I watched one day as some chickens waddled their way into the hole, clucking and squawking. It was a farm, there were chickens all over, but because we lived off the land it was important to take advantage of all the farm's gifts, and eggs were an important commodity in those days, a precious resource. The chickens had gone deep into that hole to lay their eggs, out of our reach.

When I saw those chickens I didn't even think about it before I took action. Little did I know what was about to happen!

I didn't think too much about it but felt very brave as I grabbed a lantern and lit it. The lanterns on our farm weren't the ones with the glass sides, either—it had an open design so that the wick and its flame, once lit, could easily be touched or set something on fire. I crouched down and started making my way down that hole amid the stacks of straw, trying to crawl as I carried the lit lantern.

As I made my way down that prickly, dark shoot it never occurred to me that I was doing something dangerous and possibly deadly. I was just determined to accomplish my task. Somehow I made it to the end of the tunnel and scooped up all the eggs without the lantern setting the bundles surrounding me ablaze.

But I was not so lucky on the way out. The lantern

fire managed to kiss the bales of straw and suddenly, things got very hot. I scurried back out with myself and all the eggs and when I was just a foot away from the opening, tossed the lantern out ahead of me, using my legs and arms to get out of there as quickly as I could. Miraculously, only my hair was singed but tragedy was only narrowly averted. Had I been any slower in making my way out, I would have been seriously injured or killed. The whole area quickly went up in flames, cooking some of the chickens who had decided to use the area as a nest.

A crew had been working on railroad track nearby, and as the fire began to intensify they arrived to help battle it. Thankfully the only victims of the fire turned out to be the chickens. Years later I still feel lucky about my great escape—but I wasn't the only one who got something positive from what could have been a life-altering disaster. My sister ended up becoming friendly with one of the men from that railroad crew who had come to help us. They started dating and a few years later, they married.

My father would eventually be plagued by illness, and right at the end of the war I became aware that he was suddenly a bit older, probably because of stress. But he never wavered from his sense of morals or the lessons he wanted us to learn, and I remember clearly an incident with my brother that demonstrated my father's resolve.

I grew up in a big family with lots of kids, so fighting and noise and arguing were really pretty normal. My father would hear that arguing and he had such control of us, so much of our respect, that all he had to do was whistle and we would calm down right away.

Yet even in the best families, sometimes there is a bad element, and nothing my father did seemed to control or influence one of my older brothers. My brother, Orlando, was always a troublesome child, proof that not every flower bud is meant to bloom equally, I suppose. He was the type who seemed so lost right from the beginning of his life. As a young child Orlando was a troublemaker who stole some grapes from the neighbors just because it made our father angry. Jealousy was a hallmark of his character from early on.

Once, I accidentally broke a thermometer or some such item. In those days, you didn't just go to the convenience store and spend a couple of bucks and pick one up. I don't remember how much it cost but it wasn't a cheap item. But it was an accident and while my father was upset, he wasn't angry at me.

Yet my brother couldn't see that it was just an accident. He broke the new thermometer on purpose. For this, my father smacked him, because it was an intentional, willful act on my brother's part. But my brother, his vision twisted by jealousy, took my father's reaction a whole different way.

"See?" he said to me. "He loves you more than me."

He was always testing my father, and always came to the same conclusion: that he was competing against me for our father's love and was always the loser.

My father didn't treat my brother any differently than the rest of us, but just as some flowers wilt in the light of the sun while others grow stronger, my brother never seemed to take my father's efforts the way they were meant to be taken.

It was just after the war. I was about eight years old and my brother was ten. It was summertime, August, quite a hot season in Italy, and we had just returned from the annual Feast of San Lorenzo, the patron saint of our town. We had gone into town that day like everybody else. There'd been big crowds, vendors selling things, food and entertainment. When we came home, my brother had a little whistle in his hand, and it caught the attention of my father.

"What's this? Where did you get it?" my father asked him.

There'd been a clown at the festival that day, in a costume with those big shoes, and the clown had been selling those small noisemakers. But my brother told my father he had gotten the whistle from a basket, had simply reached out his hand and taken it, and when my father asked if he had paid for it, my brother simply responded, "No."

Even though my brother had always caused problems, my father was relentless in his moral vision. He did not give up on my brother, holding up the moral lesson he wanted my brother to learn no matter how frustrating the child made the situation.

"You cannot keep that thing, you've got to bring it back," my father said firmly.

My mother agreed with my father, knowing it was important to teach my brother a lesson and that he could not be allowed to keep something he had stolen. But it was August and the sun was strong. She argued that the whistle could be returned later on. The trip back to town was a mile, the same road she traveled each day with her basket of produce to sell, and in the midday heat the trip would be unnecessarily taxing. But my father would hear none of it.

"You've got to go and bring it back right now," he insisted.

He was tough, but not without a heart. Just as when he'd sent me to bed without supper at age four, my father wanted Orlando to learn the lesson. My father walked with my brother for that long mile back to town in the noon heat—but it seemed my brother would never take in the light of our father's love.

I also remember that year's festival for its big fireworks show. With the end of the war the fireworks were bigger and louder than ever, and though most of us enjoyed it my younger brother, who was just five years old, was terrified. The loud booms and popping sounds created by the fireworks made him think it was the war all over again.

I'll never forget the fear on his face, which was so acute he practically turned yellow.

But it was my older brother whom I had a tough time with, always. His jealous and callous nature seemed to interfere with my life every time I turned around, from the time I was young until I was a young adult and on my way to a life in America.

My brother would constantly try to instigate fights or beat me up, and while brothers and sisters always roughhouse with each other, his actions seemed to hold a bit more venom. I often played by myself, in part because he would come by and dash apart anything I was playing with.

In those days they were just starting to introduce electricity to my region of Italy. I would watch those crews work, digging holes into the ground, putting in the tall poles, stringing the wiring in between. Sometimes when I would play I would mimic that, digging holes and twisting tiny wires together between sticks to form my own little electric line. In my play I even created little housing developments. I guess that all along some part of me knew that I wanted to be a builder, even if I couldn't articulate it!

My brother would come by and tear everything I had made during play apart so quickly I couldn't stop him. He never seemed to care.

I usually kept to myself and kept quiet, maybe because of the way Orlando would treat me. But there was another kid in the neighborhood who seemed determined to make my life hell. The boy, who lived a few blocks away, was a bully to everyone but he loved to target me.

I was so happy to be going to school again after the war, but around the fourth grade this bully always tried to beat me up. I would be walking to school in the morning and the bully would appear—threatening and teasing, trying to scare me.

Usually, I was able to ignore him and just keep walking. This boy, really, there was nothing special about him. He was average in every way, from an average family, and wasn't even much bigger than I was at the time. But I was timid and never fought back, and I would do anything I could to avoid a confrontation.

The boy might have been disturbed in the head, too. One morning he didn't just bully me with words or by pushing me around. He approached me wielding a sharp sickle in his hands, and I was frozen in fear, terrified. I can't even remember if I actually went to school that day or how I got away from him.

My brother, who usually solved all his problems with his fists, could not understand why I let that boy bully me. My brother would say to me over and over, "Why don't you just beat him up?" But I never would.

So my brother decided to "help" by doing things his way. He began to spread rumors that I was planning on fighting the bully, telling everyone that there was going to be a big match between us.

Thanks to my brother's handiwork, the bully confronted me one Sunday afternoon and started pushing me around, taking swings at me too. Except for a few of his friends and my brother, who was watching from far away, we were pretty much alone despite a dance that was being held nearby.

The bully had only gone so far up to that point and had never actually hit me before. But my brother's rumor-mongering had inspired the boy, and he punched me.

Something welled up inside of me—a feeling so strong and overwhelming that I couldn't ignore it or avoid the confrontation anymore. I finally snapped. Something fierce inside of me could no longer be pushed around or stay silent while I was being abused. I grabbed that bully with a fury I didn't even know I had and put him in a headlock.

I began punching at him so hard and strong it was like I was trying to knock his nose off of his head. The blood was pouring from his nose and it got everywhere, including on my clothes and on the ground.

The violence that erupted from me lasted so long,

my brother finally stepped up. He had to take that boy off my hands and separate us before I would stop punching. I wasn't proud of myself. I didn't like to fight, and didn't like being the center of attention. That fight accomplished a few things, though. I never saw that bully again. I'm sure he was around, since he lived in the neighborhood, but he never crossed my path after our battle.

And after that? My brother stopped beating me up too. It's not as if he started treating me with respect or stopped trying to mess with me altogether. But watching me fight back made him think twice about using his fists on me.

The bullying ended, and then school did too. The nearest school that did have classes was miles away, but my father had begun to feel ill, his sciatic nerve becoming painful and making walking an ordeal. His sickness made it impossible for us to get to school, and the whole idea of us continuing on was simply abandoned.

My father's illness was tough to bear. This was a man who, just a few years after the war, when resources were scarce, would think nothing of riding a bike ten miles away to another town to get us school books, a man who had been a farmer his whole life.

There were signs of how serious his illness was to become, but we didn't really know it at the time, and medicine then was not what it is now. In fact, I can clearly remember neighbors of ours, skilled in home remedies, using leeches to help ease my father's pain.

There was one day, toward the end of the war, when we were all at the table in our house in Piglio, eating. Without warning, my father passed out; I can still see my oldest brother, just eighteen years old, leaping up and catching our father before he fell to the ground. We had no way of knowing then that his collapse that day was a warning of the tumor that was growing in his brain.

But at the age of twelve, I didn't comprehend the full impact of my father's illness. I did understand, with a deepening dread, the negative impact that my lack of education could have on my life and future.

The point was only brought home all the more by my aunt and uncle, who would buy wine and olive oil from my parents and then sell the goods to people in Rome. They used to talk to us all about school and education, which only served to further my anxiety.

My inability to continue my schooling gnawed at me. I became morose and distracted, and at twelve years old found myself seriously contemplating my future. My father was a farmer, and his father before him, but I was not so sure that life was for me.

I thought about becoming a priest, but in those days it was tough to go to seminary because you had to be a somebody to get into seminary, but especially because one needed more than a fifth-grade education, so I quickly dismissed the idea of being a priest.

When you're a child like that your mind wanders, and I was always thinking, *What am I going to do when I grow up? And without an education, what am I going to do?*

I became lazy about that time; nobody could get any work out of me. I became a bit of a family joke even though I still did farm chores, helping to gather things for the cows and other daily tasks. But I was easily distracted, and not too motivated. My family would poke fun, saying I wasn't all that good at working but was a champion eater, and the first at the dinner table.

Always, in the back of my mind, I wondered what I would do with my life.

One day, as I thought about the question, something changed—I had a vision. It was as if my constant thinking and consideration of my future suddenly culminated in a single, visual idea.

I saw a great tree before me, in my mind's eye. The tree was huge, with many branches reaching out into the sky, and I that knew on each of those branches was one of my wishes—all the possibilities for the years that lay ahead of me, like a road map.

I saw a bright future on each branch, in every way that I turned. I saw myself as a restaurant owner, a bus or truck driver, a farmer, a teacher or priest—though, again, as I thought it over I realized that the lack of education would only hamper any effort to become a teacher or priest. I knew I had to eliminate those options.

And the more I thought, the more I knew I didn't want to be a farmer. I loved and respected my father, and knew my parents provided for us very well with farming, but I felt it didn't suit me. It took too much work, and too long, before the fruits of one's labor could be enjoyed, or before one saw any profit. So, I scrapped that choice pretty quickly.

Then I saw it: a spot in my vision so bright, I couldn't ignore it. It was a little, bright dot, very far away at the end of one of the branches of that great tree. I didn't know what it was, but I knew it was my future and it made me pray to God to help me understand.

I had so much faith in God, but I was young and trying to figure out what to do with my life. When there are obstacles in your way, or you can't find the answers you need, it's easy to lose hope.

I found myself always hanging around construction sites, watching the workers, just like when I was a child and would observe the crews who were putting up electrical poles. Building and construction seemed to always draw my attention like a magnet, and I loved being there, even though no one in my family was in construction.

I knew I loved being around construction sites but I had yet to truly understand the possibilities that love represented. Then, one day, my vision came to mind again. I saw the great tree and its beautiful, bright branches. I saw the limb with my future at the end, shining hotly, and finally knew what it meant.

I'm not sure where my love of building comes from or what inspired it. Perhaps it was watching the damage done by the war, or maybe it was just something that was always inside of me. But at that moment I knew I wanted to be a builder, to make homes.

It felt like God was trying to let me know he had heard my prayers. My faith was like a seed that had been planted and was beginning to grow. While I was relieved that the monumental decision had been made, I felt at once frustrated and angry because my situation had not changed. Being a builder would not be easy, especially with key ingredients like education missing, and at that time I thought it was impossible to get the skills I needed.

The more I thought about the things in my way, the more my faith in God and my dreams began to waver, the more hope began to fade again. If my faith was a seedling, it needed some nourishment. As time went on my faith, my vision and my belief in God were struggling—but the dream wouldn't go away. It was as if God were a light in my mind, and while the light dimmed, it never did go out.

What I didn't understand then was that education is not the only thing a person needs to become successful in life. There is a difference between being intelligent and achieving academic success, and there have been many people who've become great entrepreneurs without traditional educations.

We don't always realize our dreams right away. And life was going on at the farm, where we were all expected to do our chores and routines. But there is always change, and like in nature, sometimes a change means the ending of something.

My grandfather was still a spry, slim man, never without his trusty shotgun as he roamed the mountains near the farm he'd known since he himself was a teenager. In many ways it seemed as if he were a tall, strong, ancient tree, his massive presence so deeply rooted in our family that life couldn't be imagined without him there.

He had explored the hills around Piglio since his youth, hunting and herding, learning the land that was to become his own.

When my grandfather was young, the land had been owned by his uncle, who was fairly rich for the times. The uncle was in the transportation business and owned quite a bit of land. He had bought sixty cows and used to set them out to graze in an area about ten miles away from our farm.

There was a big forest there, in the region of Italy known as Lazio, and in the spring they would bring the cows up the mountain to pasture for the summer in the lush, green hills. Even though everyone usually branded their cows so that they could be identified, once the bovines were set loose to feed like that they would often get mixed up, and people had to sort out which ones belonged to whom. My grandfather was just a kid but he would often help his uncle with the animals and spent a lot of time with the older man.

One year, the uncle was almost fatally injured when the horse he was riding was spooked, throwing the man off. My grandfather's help became even more valuable.

The uncle had never married, and did not have any children. And as the uncle got older, he became resentful of his brother-in-laws and felt that they were only waiting around for him to die, so they could lay claim to his land and to his money. The thought of that made him quite angry.

He went to his brother, my great-grandfather, with a proposal.

"I'd like to adopt your son," the uncle said. "And if I adopt him, I'll leave everything I've got to him."

It was a startling idea and not one that my great-grandfather was eager to capitulate to. But after a lot of thought and some time, they eventually agreed and made it a legal arrangement, with the uncle adopting my grandfather at the age of sixteen.

Some might say my grandfather was lucky to be chosen in that way, and to be in line for his uncle's fortune, but I don't think my grandfather ever saw it only in terms of the money. He just wasn't that type of person.

At sixteen he got a hunting license, and he would go out with his uncle into the mountains, hunting together. The uncle was quite a religious man, and in those days Bibles were not plentiful, but when he did die, one of the things the uncle left my grandfather was a book of scripture. My grandfather's copy of *La Sacra Scrittura*, or the sacred scripture, sort of an edited version of the Bible, was still around when I was a child.

My grandfather knew that land better than almost anything else and raised his own family there and watched as his son raise us there. He was a pillar of strength in our family through good and bad times.

But even the strongest of trees cannot last forever, and there is one day, I remember quite clearly, when my grandfather had gone on his usual jaunt up the mountain to cut and gather a particular plant that our donkey just loved to eat. He came down with a bundle of that stuff on his shoulder, but on that day I noticed he was out of breath.

After that my grandfather put down his shotgun. He stayed closer to home. It was almost as if he knew what might happen. I know the doctor gave him some medicine; I believe now that his affliction was some kind of blockage in his heart, and if he'd had that today he probably could have lived another ten years. But in those times, the doctors' medicine just wasn't enough. I was about thirteen when my grandfather died.

I don't really remember too much about my grandfather's death, perhaps because it was so painful to lose someone I loved so much and knew so well, maybe just because it was many years ago. But at that age, time does its job, going on by itself and in the end dulling the heartache. I still miss my grandfather and think of him fondly, but at that moment we had to just keep going on and stay busy with the farm, since there was no school.

There were more changes in store, and when I was sixteen years old my family moved away from the farm in Piglio to Anzio in central Italy, near Rome.

My parents were still farmers, and they sold the property in Piglio to a relative so that the land that had already been in my family for generations still, to this day, is. But it was thought that farming this new property might be easier work, with its sandy soil. While the soil was easier to work with, the fruits and vegetables it produced were often not as good as those born from the land in Piglio.

After our family moved, a contact helped me get my first job at a construction site. I was excited and felt a newfound sense of purpose that alleviated the anxiety that had been clouding my mind and heart for so long.

The family joke at that time was that I was lazy, but you wouldn't know it judging by my first day of work. The workers were pouring concrete for the first floor of a house, and it was my job to carry buckets of cement to workers who needed it. I was one of four or five guys who would carry the cement. I hauled the heavy buckets over my shoulder, up one flight to the man working with it. Back and forth, all day long I carried those weighty buckets and even though this was much harder work than almost anything I had done on my parents' farm, it didn't bother me.

I wasn't bothered by the labor because I loved the work so much. It made all the difference in the world and gave me a sense of peace and security, like a plant or flower whose roots have become well-established.

When plants are well-rooted and have a strong foundation, they can only grow taller or stronger. When we allow our faith in God and ourselves to bloom, we are the better for it.

I had asked God to guide me, to show me the way to my future, and though it took time I was able to find that path. However, those first few days were not without problems.

After a day of carrying those buckets full of cement, I was so tired that every bone in my body ached. Though I had finally found my motivation, I wasn't used to such physical labor and it was painfully clear in my body's reaction.

The next day at work, around two p.m., the construction crew had reached a certain point in the work and the boss let everybody stop for the day and relax, because the job had been finished. It was a bit of a party for the rest of the day, with all kinds of goodies like salami, prosciutto and very good bread. That's the way they would celebrate when they finished building a floor of a house: They would raise a flag and have a party or a good time.

But I couldn't enjoy the socializing. I didn't know what was wrong, but I was quite sick and everything felt like a struggle. I thought my body just wasn't acclimated to such physical work.

I skipped the partying and tried to go home, but the walk was torture. It was less than a mile away, and while most people today might think that's a far walk, it's really not. In those days we walked everywhere and I was used to it, but on this day I could barely move. It took me more than an hour to get home; every step took tremendous effort.

When I finally arrived, my mother had to put me to bed. She sat up next to me all night, using a wet rag to keep my forehead cool. The next day we went to see the doctor. That's when I found out that I wasn't just a lazy guy who had to get used to hard work—I actually had pneumonia. The doctor gave me some medicine and a few days later I was recovered, and I went back to work.

In my first few days and weeks of work I assisted a master builder who was making a staircase. He was using mortar and measuring so precisely, and he knew every step by heart. I watched him work and knew that I needed to do something to get more education.

I had to do something to help myself. I decided to take action and found my fifth-grade schoolbooks to teach myself as much as I could, learning as much reading and multiplication and division as I was able to. Mastering the simple math proved to be easy, but I was frustrated because I couldn't do more.

In those days I was never without my paper and pencil, and every spare moment I had was spent with those books. My brother, Orlando, would make fun of me, but I didn't care. I never wasted a moment.

At that time I was just starting to really become aware of the world around me. I used to stop at the bar near the train station in Lavinio—which, in Italy, is not really a bar like it is in America but more of a neighborhood café or gathering spot. I would stop in from time to time, and I remember hearing a rumor about a couple from the neighborhood.

As the story goes, the man had always been very proud, living off his father's money. But then he met and married a woman and they had a child together. It was then that the man realized that he was ashamed to be using his father's money to support his child.

The man decided to get a job and ended up finding work that took him away from home—to France and Germany.

But instead of being proud of him, his wife ended up cheating on him, fooling around behind his back. I didn't know the couple personally, but hearing those stories sent a chill through my heart. I didn't usually ask God for anything specific; I always believed it was better to simply pray to God, not to make demands on him. But after I heard about this couple, I begged God not to give me a wife like that man's wife—I wanted a good wife, a good-hearted woman.

In those days, though, I wasn't really about to get married. I didn't even have a steady girlfriend; I was more focused on work and educating myself. But I could only work with the construction company in the winter months, when the farm life was slower. But the work gave me money to pursue another newfound passion: bicycle racing.

I was not exactly a natural athlete, and my love of eating didn't help, but I could handle a certain amount of physical work and labor just by virtue of my age and energy. I was about seventeen years old when I took up bicycle racing, which at the time was a very popular sport in Italy. There were teams and leagues, and people used to race competitively, and the pastime was so popular they would print the results of the contests in the newspaper, sort of like football or baseball in America.

All the kids dreamed of being successful, competitive bike riders but few actually made it. I used to go bike riding for two or three hours a week and I was able to use the money from my construction job to pay for a nice racing bicycle. I joined a team and competed, but never even won a race.

The course we used to race on was a steep, zigzagging mountain road. The path would go for a few miles in one direction before making a sharp turn and bringing the rider back in the other direction, the incline increasing all the way. But it was fairly easy to simply cut out large sections of the course by avoiding some of the zigs and zags, going off the path and heading straight up the mountain.

During one race what I thought was a clever idea came to mind: I decided to use a shortcut. I got off my bike and carried it, running up to the next section of the course on foot. I thought I could get ahead that way, and there were no coaches out on the road with us to watch or dissuade us from doing such a thing.

Boy, did I learn a lesson that day. Of course, I got caught trying to cheat. It was such an embarrassing moment. I was cut from my team, and my coach was furious with me. Instead of getting my name printed in the paper for doing well in bicycle racing, I was disqualified for the rest of the summer, and that surely made the papers!

For all the pain and shame I felt from getting caught, in many ways it was a blessing. Just as when I was four years old and my father sent me to bed without supper, I learned something that day that forever shaped my character: I learned how useless cheating is.

I know if I hadn't gotten caught, if I had won that race by cheating, it would have been no good. You don't want to be a hero by lying. That kind of action is akin to a shiny apple that looks delicious on the outside, but is hiding a worm on the inside—at the core, it's rotten. That's not the kind of hero or person I wanted to be. Getting caught that day helped me realize that and helped me stay on a path of honesty, one that serves God's will, even to this day.

I kept racing for two more years, but really it wasn't for me. The lesson stuck with me, though, and I never tried to cheat or distort things to my advantage ever again.

In many ways I was a typical teenage boy—working, bike racing, helping my parents and developing an eye for the girls. I would do my construction work and was always trying to meet girls, trying to decide which one was the best looking.

Then, one day, this young girl caught my eye. She would ride back and forth on her bicycle, delivering eggs from her family's farm to customers. She was around fourteen years old and had a beautiful smile, but it wasn't only her looks that drew me in. She was just different. It's tough to explain, but she was like the wind—she never stopped. She never even said "hi" or acknowledged me, but I was intrigued by her.

Sometimes I would try to talk to Maria, but once she learned that I was interested, she stayed away, flying off on her bicycle as if I wasn't even there and never giving me a chance to talk to her or get to know her. She would walk away so fast, and she was so skinny, always wearing these long skirts full of material that would swirl around as she walked. She was like a butterfly that couldn't fly straight but was always bouncing here and there.

I couldn't take my eyes off of her, but it was tough to even introduce myself. I was having a difficult time getting Maria's attention, but at work I was doing quite well, and my boss had taken a liking to me. At that age, I was like a bull: I could work all day long and nothing would bother me. He showed me how to do specialized work, training me in a variety of tasks and different parts of home construction. First was the underground plumbing in a house, a critical feature.

I was able to do everything the boss had shown me almost perfectly, and in a short amount of time. At the end of the day the boss trusted me and I was left to perform that important work on many other construction jobs for him.

He was smart in a way, too, because he never paid me any more for doing such a unique task, so he saved himself money. I was a sort of an apprentice, and I learned how to do other things like hanging doors and creating ceilings and terra cotta elements.

I worked there for a few years and even though I wasn't getting paid what I should have been, I was gaining something, too. I found I could learn a lot just by watching how people worked. I discovered a natural ability with construction, an affinity for each task. The more work I did, the more I enjoyed it and the more comfortable I became both with the work and with my boss.

Maria was still a mystery to me. She was a fun girl, very interesting, and I thought about her a lot. I would try to say "*ciao*" and she seemed to understand that I was interested in her but she would have none of it.

One day I was walking in the street. She rode up next to me on that bicycle she was always riding and I must have called out to her. She whipped around and stopped, looking at me.

"I know what you're looking to me for," she said coolly.

I think I was a bit shaken, and I replied, "Yes." But Maria wasn't cutting me any slack.

"I don't want to be your girlfriend," she said.

I protested and told her that I'd never said any such

thing, but she just ran away again. I didn't want to scare her but God knows I tried very hard to build a relationship with her.

Sometimes we need to be patient, to take our time and work hard at something before God recognizes our efforts and we are rewarded. In nature some of the most difficult plants to grow are among the most beautiful, and my courting of Maria was a bit like that. It took a lot of time and careful, delicate effort. I had to get this just right.

The next year it became a bit easier. She slowed down a bit and wasn't so quick to run away. At that time Maria was going to learn how to be a seamstress in a shop that made women's suits and bridal gowns. She walked there. She was growing up, not such a little girl anymore.

I saw my chance one day, and after having spotted her from far away I approached, walking close by her.

"*Ciao*. How are you doing?" I said. And this time, though she didn't welcome me with open arms, she didn't run off right away either.

"*Ciao*," she said, and kept going.

"I'd like to talk to you a little bit," I said.

"I already told you I don't want to be your girlfriend," Maria huffed. "So what's the use?"

By then, I was a bit older myself and could handle myself a bit better. I laughed at her rebuff.

"Not only girlfriends and boyfriends talk. Everybody does," I said.

She didn't run away at all. In fact, we talked for about twenty minutes that day, until she had to go. It was like a victory for us even though we didn't know it then.

Another day I saw her again because I knew the route she took and where she was going to go by, and I was always sort of watching out for her. I approached again, and she wasn't hostile. In fact, she stuck around and we talked for forty-five minutes that day.

Suddenly, she jumped up, realizing the time, and blurted out, "My mother is going to kill me."

She started to run, flying fast as her skirt swirled. Then she just as suddenly stopped. Maria turned around and came back over to me.

"You know," she said slowly. "Nobody ever talked to me like you do."

Then she left again. But I knew that she was starting to feel the same about me as I did about her.

I tried not to bother her too much, but I had succeeded in making a connection with her. Once in a while Maria would come by and we would chat. I tried to have some fun one day and told her I wanted to ask her something.

"So," I said. "You don't love me?"

"No, why do you ask me that?" she said.

"So, I want to ask you another question: Do you hate me?"

"No, you're a nice guy," she said. "Why would I hate you?"

"Shoot!" I joked.

"Why? What?" she said, looking a bit confused.

"Well, it's easy to change a big hate into a big love."

We both started to laugh, and at that moment we both knew. Things had started to change in our favor. The more I got to know Maria, the more I realized that what I was feeling for her was more than just a good feeling; it was actually very special. And I think that when she began paying attention to me, she felt the same way.

But our love was just beginning to bloom, and in the fall of that year she left with her family for America. We were apart for quite some time, two and a half years to be exact. It wasn't so easy to call at that time; we couldn't zip messages to each other through a computer. We spent all that time writing letters back and forth, staying connected and building our relationship.

It was tough for us to be apart, but I was certainly staying busy at work, where I continued to soak up knowledge about and experience in building homes. I became quite confident in my work and happy with my job.

After I started working, I could see even more

clearly the possibilities for my future and I believed that I could succeed. I was learning who I really was and I knew that I never had to quit anything because of a lack of knowledge or any laziness on my part. When I started something, I always found a way to break through the obstacles and finish.

One day the boss was talking with me, and we were having such a nice conversation. I was feeling so good and so happy, I told him, "I'm going to be in business just like you."

I meant it both as admiration of him and as an expression of happiness and confidence in my new-found passion. But that simple, innocent admission of mine changed my relationship with my boss, and not for the better. He wasn't flattered or happy for me. Instead, from that day on, he didn't let me lay a single brick or do any of the things I had been doing. He treated me differently, more coldly, and suddenly I was shunned by the man who had opened this world up to me.

I think he took my admiration and confidence as a threat and believed that one day I would become his competition. It was a shame, but it did not really matter. I had found my roots in a love of construction, discovered a passion within me for the work, and now I had the experience under my belt. I was growing stronger with each task and the roots were too strong for anyone's discouragement to disrupt.

But my ability to branch out and allow those roots to really take hold was disrupted, and I was shaken to my very core by a stinging, deep loss.

While I'd been growing up, discovering my passion and finding love, my father had been on a different path. In that decade he had begun what was at first an almost invisible decline, just a little bit at a time in a way that was persistent but hard to fully comprehend. It was as if he were a sun whose brightness was slowly being obscured by clouds, becoming a little less intense as time went on.

My father was losing his memory and, it seemed, his will a little bit as well. He was seeing doctors regularly. Terrible headaches had developed and he was living in great pain until finally the doctors diagnosed his brain tumor. After a lot of discussion, they decided the only thing to do was operate.

Brain surgery in the 1950s wasn't on par with today's medicine. It was a big risk that my father decided to take, but his pain was so unbearable, he knew he had to do something.

We would visit him in the hospital regularly, a handful of us going at once to share the time and ease the burden. I was nineteen.

Our father's illness seemed to unleash something in my older brother, Orlando, who was just twenty-one years old. The more sick my father became, the bossier and more out of control Orlando seemed to get. He constantly accused the rest of the family of not being able to do anything right and attempted to intimidate me and our sisters. He even threatened one of our older brothers.

He seemed to see our father's decline as an opportunity to use our family to get whatever he wanted, all with a perspective that just seemed twisted. When we sold our farm in Piglio to my aunt, it was Orlando's responsibility to go to the bank and pick up the check. They gave him a cashier's check worth two million lira, or the equivalent of a few thousand dollars. It was a significant sum of money in those days.

Somehow, Orlando thought picking up that check made that money his. It was a baffling and unwelcome sideshow during one of our darkest times.

As for myself, without the guiding star of my father's love and wisdom, I felt just a little bit lost. One day, I went to the hospital by myself to see my father. I didn't talk to anyone about it or tell anyone I was going. I left the house and made the trip by bus to the hospital.

I so badly just wanted to see him, to talk to and be with the father I loved so much. And talk we did—for so many hours that after we were done I couldn't remember all we'd discussed.

Some of it was things every young man should hear from his father. He encouraged me always to tell the truth and talked about integrity and honor. Other times, he was concerned for my mother and younger siblings, telling me what I needed to do to help them and take care of them.

It was quiet, just the two of us talking, but the sadness in the room was palpable. He had a sense of the dangers ahead of him and how risky the surgery was.

"Maybe I'm not going to make it. I'm not sure I'm going to make it but I cannot live like this anymore," he said.

The pain had become too great at that point and he knew he had to do something, so there seemed no choice but for him to undergo the surgery.

We kept talking. I wanted to get every minute that I could with him, soak up all the love and knowledge and wisdom that I could. I didn't want to leave. I had been there for hours by the time they announced the end of visiting hours but I didn't pay any attention.

The nurse came by, saw that I was still there and yelled at me to leave. Reluctantly, my father walked me down the hallway and to the door of the hospital, but we were still talking forty-five minutes later, when the nurse passed by again. She yelled again, telling me to go home, and this time took my father by the hands to lead him back to his room.

He was a little bit forgetful at that point, and he was trying to remember something that he wanted me to know, but we had been talking about so many things. As the nurse was leading my father away he suddenly stopped just two or three steps away from me, as if he finally recalled the one thing he wanted to tell me.

"In other words, never make God mad," he said before the nurse finally got him to his room.

I left, returning home on the bus, and even though I had spent so much time with my father it seemed like it wasn't enough. He died the next day. My idol, my teacher, my friend—all of a sudden he was gone.

My whole family was rocked to the core. It was as if our family was draped in the darkness of an eclipse that blocked out the sun, and the loss of my father's energy, love and guidance was a threat to us all.

I remember my younger brother, Natale, sitting around on the sidelines, looking as if he had died too. And it seemed as though he was like that for the longest time. My mother was shaken; she was so low. But my father had died on June 12, right in the middle of one of the farm's busiest times, and so she never gave up. She always tried to be strong. Despite her terrible loss, my mother continued her long, grueling, daily trips to the market. She didn't miss a thing.

I coped as best as I could. I kept working and doing all the things I had done before, including trying to educate myself. But I was in a fog. I couldn't remember most of what my father and I had talked about in those final hours, and it made my heart ache.

Even though on the outside I appeared okay, on the inside I felt lost and confused. I struggled to come to terms with my father being gone just as I was trying to build my future.

And Orlando didn't help. Nothing seemed to straighten him out, not even sixteen or seventeen months of serving in the army. He bought so many supplies for the farm that he racked up all kinds of debt for our family—debt that my poor mother had to end up paying off. He was always trying to bully us, his brothers and sisters, into giving him ownership of the property that our family had purchased, because each of us had a portion of that land in our own names.

It was a difficult time for all of us. I had never seen my mother suffer like that. There was one day when she was so worried, she didn't know what to do. When my father died the family had so much debt, we decided to sell two or three of the lots in our names, and we used the money from that sale to pay off what we owed. Everything should have been OK after that, but it wasn't.

When Orlando got home from the army, the experience hadn't changed him or made him less selfish. When he got home he could have just worked, supporting himself and living his life, but he made a different decision. He went back to his same old habits, purchasing with abandon and buying whatever he wanted. And even though he was buying grains and seeds and fertilizer for the farm and it could appear that he was trying to do a good thing, he never used those things in the correct way, and never was able to cultivate the products of the farm. He didn't seem to care that his actions were hurting other people, especially his own mother and family. Before my mother knew what to do she was facing another mountain of debt. Even though it was Orlando making the problems, he often tried to dupe our mother into taking responsibility.

One night I was in the kitchen with my mother, and she was in despair.

"What are we going to do now? There's all this debt to pay," she moaned as she prepared supper for the whole family.

I told her that she could not sign any more paperwork any for Orlando. He used fear and intimidation and, when he had to, he just lied to our mother to get what he wanted. She said she thought that she had been signing "applications," but she didn't understand that signing those applications was the same thing as signing a legal note that made her responsible for the debts that should have been Orlando's problem. I begged her not to sign anything anymore, to resist any pressure from him and not believe what he said.

What I didn't know was that Orlando had been listening behind the door of the kitchen. My mother and I were on one side of the kitchen and she had a finished dinner laid out on the table, waiting to be eaten.

But Orlando didn't like my interfering with his affairs, and he didn't like what he was hearing. He burst from behind the door with such violence it was unbelievable.

"What are you doing, talking behind my back?" he raged.

He showed that night why my mother's fear of him was justified. In a blind fury, he picked up the table and threw it at my mother and me.

No one was physically harmed, and Orlando later claimed that he'd meant to throw the table only at me, not our mother. But the damage was done; his anger was practically abusive, his actions totally unjustified and without reason.

He ran out after his horrible display, and I went to go after him to fight him. But my mother stopped me, putting her hand on my chest and holding me back.

"Let him go," she said. "Let him go."

My shaken, tired mother spoke as the dinner she had slaved to make lay in ruins all over the kitchen. It was clear that Orlando was wrong, but my mother didn't want to see anyone fight, and she knew that if we fought and I somehow got arrested, it would spell big trouble for me.

She had been through enough, and I didn't want to make things harder for her so I stayed where I was. But Orlando's selfish ways weren't the only troubles we faced in the wake of our father's death.

At one point, we learned that my father's death might have been the fault of those at the hospital. My older sisters and brothers had a meeting and talked about suing the hospital because there was a rumor that a doctor had made a mistake while preparing our father for surgery, or that someone had fed him despite an order to the contrary.

But I wouldn't hear of it. It seemed to me that anything we could or would recoup from such an effort would simply be blood money. But at that age, I didn't think about what any such money could have done for my mother, who still had young children at home. I just thought of one thing.

"You do whatever you want," I told my siblings. "If you sue and get money, I don't want any part of it. I'm not going to take any enjoyment from my father's death. I don't want anything."

I continued to be down inside, and to beg God to help me understand how I should proceed after the loss of my father. Until he died, I had only known that my parents loved me; after, I started to understand that there was something else that had been eluding my grasp.

The more I thought, the more I realized that love was more than something automatic, or easy—even the love of my father. Love was also about respect, honor and responsibility. Like nature's beauty, love isn't an accident but something to be earned and worked for. Just as plants must draw on the nutrients in the soil and soak in the water and sunlight to grow, love must be nurtured and cared for, and the best people understand that.

One day it hit me, and I not only remembered my father's last message but felt like I had discovered a nugget of truth so rich and powerful, it sustained me, and still does today. I remembered and understood my father's message: "Never make God mad." I knew that it meant that I had to live my life for God, in a way that honored and respected him, and always do the best that I could do. I had to live for the pleasure of God.

I'd struggled for a long time. Now, I finally remembered what my father had been trying to tell me, and I knew how important it was, but I was just nineteen. I didn't think I could make a promise like that and keep it. I fought for a long time within myself about whether I could really handle a commitment that meant that I was dedicating myself to God's will.

At some point, my path became clear and the clouds that had darkened my soul began to lift. I stopped hesitating, and I said, "God, I promise you that I'm going to do the best that I can." I really meant it.

It was a turning point for me because I also knew that I had to strike out on my own when it came to my work in construction. Relations with my boss had become so strained, I finally had to strike out on my own and leave the construction company.

It was tough, but I started going around and finding little jobs to do on my own. I would see a pothole on a road near someone's house or a problem with their property and would approach the homeowner and ask if they wanted me to fix it. I did good work and made good money with lots of little jobs like that.

I also built walls, like small fences, around people's property—a customary thing in Italy. I'd go out with three or four other guys and do the work. By the time I was twenty-three years old, I'd gotten my first contract to build a house.

Around this time things also began to get a bit easier because Maria, my Maria, returned from America after so many months away. We had been writing letters back and forth but now we could really get to know each other, and we decided to marry.

It was a happy time but it was so clear how underestimated I was, how little people thought of me. Even though I was doing all those jobs and earning money, people still had this idea that I was lazy. My wife's uncle even cautioned her about getting married to me, telling her, "This guy doesn't like to work. He has hands like a priest. What are you going to do with him?"

Nobody had any faith in me. But we were young and in love. We didn't even care about wedding traditions in Italy, particularly the ones that said that when a couple wed, the woman's family had to bring something to the marriage like sheets, towels, blankets and other household goods. When Maria came back to Italy, she and her uncle came to my house to talk with my mother about it, and show us what Maria had to bring to the marriage.

But I told them, "What does my mother care about this? I don't care."

"Are you sure?" she said.

"Yeah. You want to know what I've got?" I said. "I've got nothing either."

Actually, what I had were my construction skills and experience, and I was able to build a partition in my parents' house, sectioning off an area so that Maria and I could have a few rooms for ourselves and live there and not pay rent. We had that. The older folks were all a bit surprised that we didn't care about the old traditions, that we weren't going to fight about anything like sheets or towels.

Our wedding was very nice, in late December 1959. We had maybe fifty people there and had hired a bus to bring everyone to the church and then back to my house. Usually it was a rainy time of year but when the bus pulled up and everybody got in, the clouds broke up, and it turned into a beautiful day. We hired the cook from a restaurant and had very nice steaks. Everybody was happy and danced the hell out of the place.

A cousin of mine who was a monk performed the ceremony. He was a much-loved man everywhere he went, and often couldn't even take a walk around town because he was so popular that everybody would stop and offer him rides.

He had had a tough time during the war and struggled to help people, including his own family. His mother was quite poor and his brothers were off fighting for the Italian army. My cousin lived in a monastery outside Piglio.

He was a bit like Robin Hood and always fought with his boss, a greedy man who was often quite rude. On Easter, the monks traditionally went around and blessed all the houses, and people would bestow precious gifts on them such as a bit of money, eggs and cheese. But my cousin would always give those gifts away to the poor instead of bringing them back to the monastery, because his boss always hoarded everything.

One Easter his boss asked him if he was going home to see his mother. When my cousin said that he was, the boss locked the pantry door to keep my cousin away from the monastery's resources. He would have had nothing to bring home to his mother. But my cousin broke the lock on the pantry door and brought a bunch of good stuff to his mother's, where they had a feast.

Of course, when his boss found out, they had a huge fight. But my cousin wasn't interested in the church's rules or his boss' interests. He was living a life that served the will of God and always made sure to follow that course.

With his blessing and help, Maria and I married, but

it was not so easy to start our happily ever after. Eventually, Maria's green card was about to expire and she was running out of time to stay in Italy. If she didn't honor its limitations, her chances of going back to America were slim because her parents were not American citizens. It was about two years into our marriage when she had to return to her family in America. She was seven months pregnant with our first child then.

At that point, I knew my future was across the Atlantic Ocean. And at that time President John F. Kennedy passed a law that helped reunite families, and my wife and I took advantage of that to help get me to America. Still, the application took more than a year to take effect.

Though it might have been obvious to some that I would join my wife and baby in America, for others it wasn't so easy to accept. My mother wept when she learned of my intentions and wondered out loud how she would be able to watch over me and make sure I was okay if I was so far away. Even though I had been working on my own and was a married man, she still felt she needed to keep an eye on me.

My brother, Orlando, was still a troublemaker too, despite all the years that had gone by. He seemed to use violence and intimidation to get what he wanted.

He tried to borrow money from me around this time and purposely wrote a bad check off my account.

That's a crime in Italy, and I was petrified that his actions would prevent me from getting the paperwork I needed to enter America. He only laughed when he saw how upset I was and thankfully, it was too minor a violation to stop my plans.

No one could really understand my decision. There was a man I used to play cards with; he was a type of philosopher, in his own way. He heard I was going to America, and he scolded me.

"This is Anzio," he said, waving his hand around at the landscape. "Look at the sunshine. This is beautiful. What the hell do you want to go to America for?"

Chapter Four

In May 1962, I said goodbye to my life in Italy. I boarded a boat, a very nice cruise ship, and spent seven days at sea, making the trip by myself and bringing along our bedroom furniture. I was twenty-six years old, going to see my wife and, for the first time, our baby. It was an exciting time.

I arrived on Mother's Day. My father-in-law and brother-in-law came to New York City to pick me up and take me five or six hours away, to a section of western Pennsylvania, where Maria and her family had settled. But before we left, I got my first taste of life in America, and it wasn't good at all.

I had eaten my breakfast on the ship and when I got off the ship in the New York Harbor, we had to wait for hours while I went through immigration and customs, and to have my box of furniture unloaded from the ship. New York was huge and quite a busy place, and I couldn't speak a word of English when I arrived, but I didn't have time to think about how intimidating it all was. I only wanted to see Maria and meet my daughter, who was thirteen months old.

We had to wait until the end of the day before we could start the journey to Pennsylvania, and we were in a business district in New York that was very busy and crowded. We decided to get something to eat, and my brother-in-law spotted a restaurant with a replica of the Tower of Pisa out front that was maybe fifteen or twenty feet tall.

"This must be an Italian restaurant," he said. "Do you want to go eat?"

We went in and sat down. It was a nice restaurant, full of people at the time. I ordered some spaghetti and meatballs. It's a simple dish and it was the kind of food I was used to back home. The man who ran the restaurant found out I had just come over from Italy. He got a little excited and said he was going to make me something special.

We sat, looking around the place. I was hungry and really wanted to eat, so when the man carried out our plates, heaped with food, and placed them in front of us, I was eager to dig in.

I don't know what he did, or what he put in the food,

but I couldn't even stand the smell. When I brought that stuff to my mouth I just couldn't eat it. It was nothing like the fresh, simple, good-quality ingredients I was used to back home. Tomatoes, a little olive oil, some black pepper—in Italy, that's all that would be put in. To this day, I'm still not sure what the man put in that meal, even though I know he was only trying to be nice.

I couldn't even stomach a few bites. I didn't mean to insult the man, but the food seemed so different from what I was used to, I just had a visceral reaction. Eventually, I wiped the sauce off a couple of the meatballs, and the man brought me some bread and a salad, and I got some food in my stomach. But that first meal was a big reminder that I was nowhere near home!

"That's the problem with America," my father-in-law said. "There is too much tax, and the food is not that good."

My father-in-law was quite pensive that day. And he had a lot to say on that trip to Pennsylvania. He gave me a lot to think about on my first day in a new country. Looking back, I can understand why. I came to America to make progress, to achieve something. But things hadn't worked out like that for him. My father-in-law, Franco, had left Italy when he was in his mid-forties and even though his family always worked hard, they didn't make a lot of money and didn't seem to have an entrepreneurial spirit. So my father-in-law was in a tough place; by the time I arrived in the land of opportunity, all he really wanted to do was go home to the old country.

Franco started asking me all kinds of questions about why I'd wanted to come to America in the first place and what I would do. I guess he thought I would end up with a job that didn't pay too well.

I told my father-in-law about my philosopher friend in Italy, the one I'd used to play cards with, and who had asked me why I would want to leave the beauty of Anzio. My father-in-law sighed and said he wished he was still in Italy.

"It's hard to get a good job here," he said.

I recalled a movie I had seen, *Un Americano in Vacanze*, starring an Italian actor. It was all about a man's journey to start a new life in America. In the movie, the son of the man took a vacation to Italy. It was made by the son of an Italian immigrant, and it had made the transition to America look so good, so appealing.

"That's just a movie. Do you really believe that?" Franco grunted. "What are you going to do? How are you going to make a living?"

He was so downbeat that day, but I wasn't deterred, and I wanted to talk to him. After all, this was the man who had helped care for my newborn daughter in her first few months, while I was an ocean away.

"I didn't come here just to get a job," I told him

frankly. "This is America—you've got to think big and reach high."

I mentioned my dreams of becoming a builder and building homes. I told him that if I couldn't find a good job, then I'd just go to work for myself. I really wasn't concerned about it; I knew that all I had to do was work hard and things would take care of themselves.

"Don't worry about it," I said. "I'm young."

But where I saw opportunity and the chance for a better life, Franco, at that time, saw a lot of tribulation. He was sort of depressed for me, though I didn't argue with him too much. I respected him.

We ended up living just outside of the city because that was where Maria's uncle had first settled when he'd come to America as a refugee, and where she and the rest of her family had been living.

When the drive from New York was over and we finally got there, it was the first time I'd laid eyes on my daughter, Gabriella, and the first time I had seen Maria in many months. They were so beautiful. Maria was sitting in the kitchen, with Gabriella asleep on her lap. I bent down and gave each of them a kiss, my precious baby giving a little smile in her sleep as I gave her a peck on the cheek. This was why I had uprooted my life and transplanted myself in a new country: for my family, and for a new future.

For two weeks we lived with Maria's family, and at the time I was very comfortable there. It was a good place to be. We ended up renting an apartment only 100 yards or so away.

It was tough to be in a new country. It took a long time before I could understand and communicate at all in English, which just sounded like noise to me. It was as if I was surrounded by singing birds—I could hear it, but I couldn't make sense of what they were saying.

But I wasn't scared or nervous, mostly because everyone was so helpful. If people had been nasty or rude when trying to communicate with me, well, then I suppose it would have been an intimidating experience, but people were really quite nice. And there were a lot of Italian immigrants in the area just like me, and it seemed like there was always someone who could translate when needed.

Not that life was trouble-free, or that every person I met had a good heart.

I had brought some of our bedroom furniture over from Italy with me, but Maria and I still needed things. Franco brought me to an Italian store in the city to buy a box spring, because that kind of thing would have been too heavy and costly to bring on the ship.

I had no idea how much these things were supposed to cost, but I was a businessman by nature and when I met the Italian man who ran that furniture store, I knew something wasn't quite right. The old man started asking me questions, but he pretty quickly stopped talking to me. He dealt with my father-in-law, and Franco struck a deal for me to pay $180 for a box spring, but I declined. I didn't have a good feeling about the situation, and something didn't seem right to me about the man at the store.

I told Maria so when I got home. She ended up going to a big department store in town and was able to get a box spring for $60, a third of the old man's price for the same item. That old man wasn't helping immigrants—he was feasting on them, really swindling people for all they had. I guess he'd realized I wasn't easy prey, which was why he'd tried to stop dealing with me.

I got my first job in June, at a tire shop. It was tough work, taking the old tires and putting new rubber and white walls onto them, and I made $1.35 an hour. It was nice in the winter because there was lot of heat involved in molding the tires and reshaping them, but it was stiflingly hot in the summer. I always had more than one job and would often perform tasks for an Italian contractor I had met, odd jobs just to earn money and keep busy.

Even though no one back home would have believed it, I wasn't afraid of hard work. I knew that to really reach my potential and have my new life take root, I had to work hard.

The first thing I did was ask my boss at the tire shop for overtime, and he said that if I wanted to, I could start work at 4:00 a.m. When I did put in the overtime, I'd wake up at 3:00 a.m. and walk more than two and a half miles to start my workday. It was tough but I was OK with it. Normally, I would grab a ride with my father-in-law, but when I worked the overtime I had to start much earlier than normal. I'd walk over an hour to bring home just $5—a lot of money in those days. And when the shop got very busy, I used to work late into the night. I remember one week when I worked ninety-two hours—and brought home $95.

But Maria and I were determined to succeed. I used to gross $54 a week and bring home $45, and still, we managed to put away $5 a week in savings. That week when I worked ninety-two hours, it was the same as bringing home nine weeks' worth of savings all at once.

I was almost always working two jobs, too, and would go to the Italian builders in the area and pick up extra jobs here or there. I couldn't speak English very well at the time, and it was easier to work with people who at least spoke the same language that I did.

I was also helping out Franco wherever I could. I had a good relationship with him, but things with my brother-in-law were not always so good. He seemed to hate me, and I had no idea why.

One of the first things I did when I arrived in America was help Franco with his house. In my spare time I would go and do odd jobs for him and fix it up a bit. I did the work for free because how could I take money from a man who had already done so much for me? I was happy to help him out.

My brother-in-law, Franco's son, lived nearby. And one day while I was working he burst into the house, looking around angrily and saying, "Where's Assunta? Where's Assunta?"

Assunta was his wife, but I had no idea where she was or why he was looking for her there. Then I realized that he must have thought I had something going on with his wife! It was one of the first times I realized how differently other people thought of me, and the experience shocked me.

I had learned my lesson about deception and cheating, about lies, and I lived my life in a way that valued honesty and hard work. I had learned those lessons so well, it never occurred to me that other people would think of me as someone who would cheat on his wife. But then I realized that it was just evil planting a seed in his mind.

Even though my bosses at the tire shop liked me and knew I was a good worker, after six or seven months I was laid off. But I never went a day without work. I filed for unemployment just once, and got a check for $18—though I never filed again. I kept doing those odd jobs for the Italian contractors and made more money. After two or three months, the tire shop asked me to come back.

At that time, and for a long time afterward, work was my top priority. There's no point in coming to America if you don't work for some progress.

I was either working or at home with my family. Maria made sure everything at home went well. She was so good; she took care of everything so that I could spend the little time I did have with my daughter, who was the very essence of my heart. I had lost the warmth and nourishment of my father's love, and I was far from the home I had always known, but with Maria by my side and the bright, young face of my daughter around, America quickly became home.

I worked for the tire shop for a year, but eventually God intervened and I was able to get a much better job at a local company. I kept the tire shop job for as long as I could, and would often run like hell from one place to the other without a moment to spare. I was determined not to waste an opportunity—or a dime.

At the time, in early 1963, I had been talking to one of my wife's cousins, and he suggested I put in an application at a local steel factory. It was a good job, one that everyone wanted to get, and I thought I probably didn't have a chance to get into the company. At my cousin's urging, I put in an application there but didn't hold out much hope. It was shortly after I'd gone back to work full-time at the tire shop.

My cousin said he knew the president of the union, and said he would talk to the union president about me. When he asked the union president to help me, it was the early 1960s, and times were tough. The union president said, "Give me his name," and my cousin wrote my name down on a piece of paper and gave it to him.

The union president put that slip of paper with my name on it in his pocket, and little did I know how close I came to never getting a job!

A few days later, the union man had a meeting with the president of the factory. The men talked for a while, conducted their business, and then were about to leave when something fell out of the union man's pocket.

"You dropped something," the company president said.

And when the union man picked up the paper and read my name, he realized that he had forgotten to mention me at all.

"Oh," the union man said, "this is my friend's cousin from Italy. Can you give him a job?"

The company president took the paper with my name on it. A couple of days later, the factory called me for an interview, and even though I couldn't speak any English at that timc, I got through it. Just a few days after that, they called me in for a physical and gave me a job.

The whole process was so quick, especially when getting hired at the factory was so competitive, that we all wondered how it had happened.

As it turned out, not even the union president seemed to know. My wife's cousin asked him how he'd gotten me a job so fast, but the man couldn't really answer. Later we found out that the company president had simply called the office and given them my name, and since I had already put an application in, he'd told them to just give me a job—even though he had never even seen me before.

But something inside of me knew that it was more than just dumb luck that had helped me get such a good job. I knew it was the helping hand of God, creating a little miracle that in the end helped ensure the direction of my life in my new country. To be sure, if I hadn't gotten the factory job, I would have just kept working as hard as I could at whatever job I could find. But it turned out that I was able to work there for years, earning decent money that allowed me to put funds aside with which to chase my dream of building homes.

This was when I truly started to see the rewards of living a life that served God, as I had promised I would a few years earlier. I had dedicated myself to my family and to working as hard as I could—and God had recognized that.

My first job at the factory was as a janitor. But it was a fast-growing company; in 1962, they were advertising and planning on adding 2,700 employees by 1970. When I tried to move up in the company they wouldn't allow me to at first, blaming it on the fact that

I couldn't speak English very well. It was true that I had trouble speaking the language, but I didn't let that hold me back.

After eight months of working as a janitor, I knew that they were looking for an apprentice machinist in one of the shops. My cousin and I went to the boss and with my cousin's help, I told the boss that I wanted to become an apprentice.

He discouraged me. The boss said that the job involved a thirty-day trial period, and that if I tried but couldn't handle the work, then I could never be a machinist again.

That was intimidating at first, but I went over and watched the workers in the machine shop—reading blueprints, setting up the machines to tap holes into the different pieces or other work. And as I watched, I realized that not only could I read the blueprints, but the work itself wasn't really that difficult. It was just like when I was younger and would hang around construction sites, absorbing the activity around me and somehow understanding it.

I decided that I was going to go for the machine shop position, and I got that job and never had a prob lem. The thirty days went by like they were nothing and I got to stay in the position. In fact, the only difficulty I had was with the union, which was always getting on my case for doing too much work!

Six months later I got a promotion and a little raise,

and after a year came another raise and promotion. In four years, I had risen to the position of first-class machinist.

There was another joy entering our lives about this time, another miracle that graced us: Maria was pregnant with our second child. Lorenzo was born in the fall of 1963.

I was working harder than ever, our family was growing and things should have been picture-perfect. But quickly, Maria noticed that something was wrong with our new son.

Lorenzo seemed as beautiful and flawless as any baby could be when he was first born. But around two, two and half months, something went terribly wrong and he developed a very high temperature. Maria called the doctor, who at first simply counseled that she should give Lorenzo a cool bath and some aspirin to help bring the fever down, but nothing she did seemed to help.

Maria became more frantic, and at first the doctor seemed to simply dismiss her concerns as the worries of a new mother. We were immigrants and were going to a doctor who didn't cost too much, and didn't exactly live around the corner. The baby wasn't getting any better and Maria couldn't contain her worry and finally the doctor realized that something was not right. He told us to bring the baby in right away, and the nurse let us in the back door so we could get in immediately, ahead of all the other people who had been waiting.

It was clear, as soon as the doctor saw Lorenzo, that quick action was needed. He told us to take our son to the hospital, and the physician called ahead so that by the time we got there, the hospital was ready for us.

They put Lorenzo, so tiny and vulnerable, so sick, in a special crib with ice to keep him cool and try to bring the fever down. It was torture to see him small, helpless and hurting.

They continued the treatment for seventeen miserable days, and for all that time the child wouldn't take any food. I visited whenever I could, often after working a 4:00 p.m. to 12:00 a.m. shift, and the nurses would let me in through a separate door so I could see him. He looked so sick.

The baby's face was skinny, not the chubby, plump cheeks they were supposed to be. His arms were skin and bones, his skin purple. He seemed unresponsive. Lorenzo was being fed intravenously, but the situation appeared grim, and Maria and I were forced to consider the unthinkable.

A very brave specialist told us that he didn't think Lorenzo would survive. The specialist told us that he was doing the best he could.

"I must tell you, though, I cannot make a miracle," he said grimly.

It was a blow to the heart that no one should have to endure. To make a baby, to wait so long for that little person to arrive, and to love him or her so much that your heart could burst from the feeling—only to have him taken so soon? Unbearable. Impossible. It was so painful we couldn't even speak.

Finally, Maria just cried. We left the hospital that January night and went home with a burden no parent should have to bear. I don't even think we talked to each other, though I do remember begging God to please give me my son, not to take him from us.

"God, I know you're taking my son back," I told him in my heart and mind, "but just because you're doing it, don't expect me to be happy. Please, allow me to weep. Even though I respect your command, it still hurts."

The heavy feeling in our hearts and in the air between us was a mix of pain and tension as we waited for the hospital to call and give us the inevitable news of our baby's death. There was no call at first, and we just ended up going to bed, each of us holding in our fear and grief.

Maria is such a light sleeper, and she always arose at four or five a.m., like a machine, to keep our household running. But that night was different. Unable to face the impending loss, we ended up sleeping the whole night through, waking up around eight in the morning with the sun streaming through the woods near our home. Then, we knew something was different.

There had been no phone call from the hospital.

No word of Lorenzo. We didn't know what could have happened or why, but we decided to go the hospital as soon as we could.

We arrived, using the separate door the nurses let me use for my visits after work. And when the nurse saw us, she just motioned with her hands for us to follow her, saying, "Come on, come on!"

We didn't know what to think. There was no hope anymore, no chance of a future with our son, and we could barely fathom what might be happening.

The walk down the hall and into the room where Lorenzo was seemed impossibly long, and we entered expecting the worst news of our lives. Then we saw the nurse with Lorenzo in her arms.

The nurse had tears streaming down her face, and she was laughing. She put Lorenzo into Maria's arms and revealed the impossible outcome.

The baby was no longer purple or frighteningly skinny and ill-looking. He was smiling and laughing; he made a nice little ball with his fist—as healthy as could be. When the nurse had come in the morning to check him, this was how she'd found him, as if he had never been sick.

Maria cradled our boy and we stared at our miracle, at God's handiwork. No one could believe the recovery Lorenzo had made, and no one seemed to be able to explain it, but we didn't care. The relief and joy was overpowering; the burden and terror were gone and the hope we thought was no longer possible soared in our hearts.

The specialist could only call it what it was: a miracle.

We left Lorenzo at the hospital just one more day, to make sure he was OK. Then we were able to take him home and, once again, our family was on its way.

From then on things were good. Gabriella and Lorenzo were healthy, I kept working hard, Maria took care of things at home and we kept saving our money. But I had come to America to achieve something more and in 1965 I knew it was time to try to make my dream a reality.

We had some money saved up, and I was able to get some money from a credit union and a loan from the bank. We picked out a piece of property and bought it, and I was quite excited and eager to start, but my in-laws started to show what they thought of me. They didn't believe I could build a house and seemed to be discouraging me. I went ahead with my plans anyway, using some of Maria's suggestions, including a front porch, a back porch and two fireplaces. It was a nice house, and quite big.

I had the motivation but I quickly found out that I needed more experience, particularly when it came to American construction methods. I knew a little bit of plumbing but had no knowledge of how to do electrical work. I needed help, so I hired part-time labor including a carpenter to build the frame, which was done in a totally different way than in Italy. In Italy carpenters don't work at all in the construction of a home.

I watched the carpenter work and hung around all the time, just so I could learn. But I did as much of the work myself as I could. I remember working so hard my body ached; I even dug the footer for the foundation, which I had to do by hand. I worked every night and on a couple of weekends at that, using a pick and digging up a couple square inches of dirt with every swing. I even woke up early on Palm Sunday, digging for two or three hours before heading to church, and I wanted to sit down so badly there because my back hurt so much. But I got the work finished, and I did a good job. People loved the work.

In the meantime, we had found out that Maria was pregnant again, with our third child. Gabriella was thriving, a beautiful little girl who, thanks to us, mostly spoke Italian before she was old enough to go to school. Lorenzo was healthy and strong. Our family continued to grow, and our children were the joy of our lives.

Finally, the weeks and months went by and the house was complete. It was beautiful—the porches, the fireplaces, hardwood floors, lots of room upstairs. No one had thought that I could do it when I'd started, and when I finished my wife and mother-in-law cried, maybe a little bit in disbelief. I was aware of that kind of negative feeling some people had about what I was trying to do, but I simply didn't pay any attention. I was so secure in myself and my dream that whenever anybody treated me like that I just got stronger. I was using the lessons I'd learned over the years, taking strength from all that my family and youth had taught me, and with my wife and kids by my side and God's guidance, I was making something good.

We tried to sell it, and kept it on the market for a few months, but no one was buying. I think some people were actually happy when I couldn't sell the house, but I ignored those naysayers.

We had to do something. We were living in the apartment, paying $45 a month in rent and paying off the mortgage on the property at $65 each month. We would go there frequently, to keep the place in order and make sure everything was OK. Soon, it was a couple of weeks before Christmas. Still, no one had bought the house. I made a decision then.

I asked Gabriella, "How would you like to live in this house?"

Gabriella was excited, and Maria heard what I said and stopped what she was doing.

"You're not kidding," she said.

It was the best choice at that time for everybody, and Maria was so happy. We all were. We moved into that house right around Christmas, and it was the best present we could have given ourselves—until our daughter, Paula, was born just a few months later. She was a feisty, healthy baby.

During all of this, I was talking to my mother, urging her to come to America and visit us. I hadn't seen her since I'd left Italy in 1962, and I missed her terribly. She had never even met my kids. But for a while, she put off the idea of making the trip.

Some might say that I'd achieved my dream then. I had come to America, found good work and built my own wonderful home for myself and my family, and I wanted my mother to see all of that, especially because I think she was still worried about me. I thank God for all the positive things that happened and believe that my choice to live in the pleasure of God is what allowed such success to happen.

When you work and live in a way that serves God's will, everything ends up working out the way it should because God takes care of you. It is a philosophy I truly believe. It is not that I prayed to God to earn a lot of money or build my first house in America before the age of thirty. I did not and do not pray for specific things or wishes. That is selfish thinking and doesn't serve the Lord. God knows more what it is that we need and what will help us, more than we possibly could. He takes care of those who do what is right by him.

I believe that God is always with us through good times and bad. Through all my struggles—learning how to communicate in English, almost losing my son to illness, working until I ached—God was by my side. He rewarded me for my faith and that is why, when I was able to finish that first home, I felt like such a success. But I didn't want to stop there. There was so much more I wanted to do. My dream was not quite realized.

But just because the desire was there doesn't mean that I was ready to follow through on my plans. Though I always worked diligently and Maria and I were saving money all along, building that first house wasn't easy, and it took a lot of our resources. Even though I now had a mortgage to pay, I was determined to continue trying to make my dream come true. I just needed the money to do it.

So, I kept working as hard as I could and as often as I could. I was still doing well at the factory and would work at the tire shop whenever I could. I also became an entrepreneur, but of a different sort that I'd originally intended: I opened a small pizza shop. I would go back and forth between all my jobs as best I could, even doing little construction jobs where I could.

For me, it was a natural instinct, and working like that was something I didn't complain about or question. I just knew that was what I had to do to get where I wanted to be, even if it meant getting up at 3:00 a.m. and walking an hour to start work, just for another $5. It is a lesson I learned from my mother, who took every opportunity and made the most of it, even if that meant grueling journeys to town on foot in the blazing sun, a heavy basket of fruit and vegetables held over her head.

Now I know it's not easy for some people to work like that, and to sacrifice in that way. It's exhausting. But for someone like my mother, she was so strong and natural at whatever she did that for her, working like that was just another chore to do. She did it because she wanted to, because the opportunity to better our family was there, not because anyone was telling her what to do. Even when my aunt discouraged her, telling her that the work was too degrading, she did it. If my mother had chosen to stop working so hard, we wouldn't have starved. She didn't make a lot of money, but what she did make made a difference and helped us.

In a way, it's an act of bravery, of heroism. A person works like that because it's better to do so than to let the opportunity pass them by.

It was a discipline that some people in America just weren't used to, I found. One time, I did a job for an older man who didn't speak too much Italian, so communicating with him was a bit difficult. He was a tough negotiator; he wanted to pay me just $1.25 an hour, a quarter less than what I asked for. Finally we agreed that I would do the work and decide on payment later. I went to his house on a Saturday and he provided me with a pick and a shovel because I didn't have any of my own. As I got started he said he had to go uptown for a little while. I just kept working away.

I got the job done pretty quickly, in just ninety minutes, and I ended up sitting on the man's porch, waiting for him. But the man got the wrong idea—he came out of his car hollering at me because he thought I had been lazing around and not doing the work.

When he realized I was actually finished with the job, he was amazed, and gave me $10.

To me, it was simply doing a job and doing it well. I always did that, even when the work wasn't really for me. I didn't own the pizza shop for long. I found it just didn't suit me, but I had given it a good effort for almost two years.

I had bought an old Volkswagen, mostly for when I went shopping for supplies for the pizza shop. That little car was good for hauling around pizza sauce.

I used to use it for construction jobs, too, when I was first starting out. I remember how one day, I was hauling around wood, two-by-fours and two-by-tens mostly, and had only used a cheap kind of twine to keep everything secure. Well, I was driving on this two-lane highway when I hit something or took a curve too fast and before I knew it, the twine had broken and the lumber spilled all over the road.

It stopped traffic and I had to get out and collect all the wood as fast as I could. It must have been a funny sight because some people were laughing as they watched, though a few were getting angry. I apologized to everyone that I could and got all the wood back onto the little Volkswagen. And, of course, the first thing I had to do then was find some good, strong rope! It was a mistake I never made again.

It was the same car we used for our first family vacation to Florida in 1969.

It was no small feat, to go on a family trip. By this time, our fourth child, David, had been born. We had two little girls and two little boys. It was a trip I'll never forget. We took the seats out of the back of the Volkswagen, loading it up with quilts and sleeping bags and other cushiony stuff all spread out. We put Gabriella, Lorenzo and Paula back there, and David sat on my wife's lap in the front passenger seat. Things were a bit different in 1969, and no one thought twice about having a child ride on their lap in the car, or about letting kids ride so casually.

Our destination was Florida, though originally I'd wanted to go to California. For a long time after I'd gotten to America, I'd thought about going home to Italy, and I really wanted to go someplace that was warm, just like it was back there. We settled on Florida because it was a little closer to Italy.

The factory would shut down each year for two weeks in July, for vacation, and that was when we took our trip. The first day we loaded up the Volkswagen and left quite early, around four a.m. We drove for a little while and when we got to Route 70 at the Pennsylvania border, it started to rain. The water was pouring down and all of a sudden I hit a puddle with the Volkswagen, and a big splash went up around the car—and inside it, too, as a gush of water shot up into Maria's face.

There was a hole in the bottom of the car I had never known about, and Maria ended up drenched. We had to stop at the first gas station we could so that Maria could dry herself off and clean up. I found some cardboard and used it to close up the hole.

That first day was a long one, but we made it all the way to South Carolina before we stopped for the night. The hotel we stayed in had a nice pool for the kids to play in, and the restaurant we ate in was good. The trip was going well, and we left again at four a.m. the next day.

On the way I stopped at a small coffee shop in a little town. I ran in to grab some coffees, chocolate milk for the kids, whatever we needed. I wasn't even really looking around me and when I got back in the car, Maria caught my attention and pointed toward the door of the coffee shop.

I raised my eyes and what I saw baffled me. There were black people waiting on benches outside, and a lady was bringing out coffee for them.

"I don't think they can go inside," Maria said.

I wasn't ignorant; I knew that racism existed. But

at that time I had never seen it for myself. I remember baseball player Willie Stargell saying, a few years later, that he would go into a restaurant with the other Pittsburgh Pirate players and there wouldn't be a place for black people. But it was one thing to know there was discrimination in the world and another thing to see it right in front of me.

I got out of the car and went back inside the shop, trying to be casual as I took a good look around. The only black people inside were the ones working behind the counter. It was such a disturbing sight; it left me with a sick feeling in the pit of my stomach. When I went back to the car, I told Maria that I had never seen anything like that. It was almost a relief to get back in the car and get away from there.

A little farther down the road, there was a tiny peach stand, one of many we passed as we drove through Georgia, and we stopped to get some. I'll never forget Maria sitting next to me in the Volkswagen, feeding a piece of peach to little David. He'd take the fruit and try to eat it but made such a mess of it, peach covering his face and dripping down his chin. But he loved it so much, we couldn't get him to stop. It was a joy to watch, and it helped us forget about the disturbing scene from the coffee shop.

We continued on the journey, stopped for some shopping, and by dark we were on Route 1 and began looking for a hotel. By the time we found one the air was buzzing, full of four-inch-long bugs including grasshoppers and all kinds of insects. The woman at the hotel rushed us inside so we could escape what felt like an invasion.

On the next leg of our trip, we got to our hotel in Hollywood, Florida, and we stayed for five days. It was a little hotel with a pool, and it was so hot—the heat reminded me of Italy. The stone on the ground around the pool was so hot it burned the kids' feet. They weren't used to such heat, but it didn't bother me.

What jumped out at me was that all around us, people were trying to buy and sell pieces of property. It was tugging at the feeling in my heart that wanted me to continue on with my dream of becoming a builder. It was like a sign from God all around me. But I wasn't about to stop and buy any land down south.

I have such fond memories of the rest of that vacation. We debated with locals about whether a side trip to Key West would be a good idea; everyone who looked at us with all those little kids, and then looked at the car, discouraged it. The children always wanted to stop for ice cream, and we usually obliged. People were very nice, including one woman in a town in Georgia who charged us just $6 for a hotel room.

We made our way home and were just a couple of miles away when little David looked up at the night sky and called out that he had just seen "a yellow banana" moon. I'll never forget his sweet face.

It was a good thing I enjoyed that trip so much. For me, it marked the last few weeks before I would once again tackle my dream. I had worked and saved as much money as I could in the years since I'd built that first house, which had eventually become our home. But even before we'd left for Florida I'd known that it was time to go ahead with my plans, with my future. I had put $50 down on a piece of property, and planned to pay $2,000 for the lot when my family and I got home.

Chapter Five

In some ways, it was easy to assume that I had achieved my American dream. I had a beautiful family whom I loved dearly. I had a good job at the factory, an opportunity many people probably envied, and one that I was lucky to get. And I had been able to build us a gorgeous home.

But there is a difference between planting a flower seed in a pot and watching it grow and bloom and cultivating a rich, colorful garden. Mother Nature gives us the tools and the example of how to live a good life. She also gives us a blueprint for a majestic life full of sweeping vistas and marvelous sights and sounds, tastes and smells. She gives us the idea and the hope for something more.

It's not an easy choice to make, but often, shooting for the highest goals brings us the greatest rewards. Just as my family was able to draw delicious fruit from trees born of the difficult farmland near the mountains in Piglio, I wanted more, even if it meant working harder than most others had to or wanted to.

I wanted a life with more than a few bursts of color, more than a handful of flowers. Just as I had told my father-in-law, Franco, one doesn't start over again in a new country unless they are dreaming big. I had come here to make something of myself, and I knew that now was the time.

While I had the vision and the motivation, it wasn't as if I hadn't already hit some roadblocks. Even though I'd spent the years since building that first house working hard and saving my money, when I went back to the bank for a loan I ran into trouble.

In the years since I'd built the first house, I'd become friendly with the bank manager. We would talk regularly and I would ask him informally about getting a loan to build another house, but he had always discouraged me. I wasn't a builder, he'd said, and they couldn't give money to just anybody. I had been given my original loan, he'd said, because they'd thought I was building a house for myself. If the banker had realized I'd been borrowing money for a house I planned to turn around and sell, he'd said it would have raised suspicions about him.

Eventually I had $5,000 saved up, and in those days it took about $15,000 to build a house. I had gone to the credit union and borrowed $5,000 from there. All I needed was another loan from the bank, but the bank wouldn't do it. All I wanted was to become a builder, but I couldn't do that without financing. It was frustrating. But as I spoke with the bank manager, he relented just a little bit—he said that if I started the project, once it got to a certain point he might be able to get me some money.

That was the kind of encouragement I needed. I then went to my suppliers and explained the situation to them—that I had this project I wanted to do but was just $5,000 short. They were agreeable and said they would work with me so that I could pay them at the end of the work.

Everything was working out. When we returned from vacation, I knew I would begin a second house.

The pleasure and comfort I got from our family vacation wasn't enough to calm my nerves once we got back. Even though I had built houses before, and even done so in America successfully, I was overcome by anxiety at the prospect of actually moving ahead with my plans.

Houses are built differently in Italy—at least they were in my day. The work is done so differently than the way it is done in America, it's like wine and water. In Italy, we build walls with stone and mortar, but over here everything is done with wood. I had never worked with a piece of wood like that before I got here. I had never even seen a circular saw. And, yes, I had already built one house here, and done so successfully, but I wasn't focusing on that accomplishment.

It was as if the anxiety and fear I felt were weeds choking all that was good in the garden of my life, obscuring my ability to see things clearly. That first night back, I started to get very sick and was so anxious I thought something was truly wrong with my body. But the truth was, I was extremely nervous because I felt like I didn't have enough experience to follow through on becoming a builder.

I felt so ill I thought I was going to die that night. Even though it was 11:00 p.m., I picked up the phone and called my friend, Angelo, an Italian who I had worked with before. He had done construction work in Italy and had been working as a contractor in America longer than I had. I begged him to come and help me, which he agreed to do with one condition.

"That's $5 an hour," he said. I agreed.

I had done the same thing while building the first house, hiring subcontractors to handle the work that I was less skilled in and watching them the whole time so I could educate myself about what they did. However, even knowing that I had some helping hands on the way didn't calm me down. I prayed to God to help me through the night, to get me through my fear so that I could achieve my goals. Eventually, I drifted off to sleep.

I had a dream that night, one of the most powerful dreams of my life. When I woke up, I knew that God had answered my prayers.

In my dream, I was back in Italy, back on the family farm in Piglio, on the hill where we used to harvest beans. But it was autumn, and there were no more beans to harvest.

When I looked at the ground all I could see were snakes. It was a terrifying sight—snakes of all kinds, slithering around and hissing, long ones and short ones, with all kinds of exaggerated features, big heads and big eyes. I was struck by fear and leapt onto a big stone to get away from them. I just sat there, trying to keep myself safe from the sinuous pile.

Out of nowhere, as it can only happen in a dream, I saw my father walking up to me. It was more than fifteen years since his death at that point, and in the intervening years I had become a father myself. Still, I missed him more than I could express.

In that moment, though, in the dream during which I was feeling so much terror, my father was the picture of calm. He walked up to me as if there were no obstacle between us, no pile of snakes waiting to attack. He came up to me and said, "What are you doing?"

"What am I doing?" I yelped, incredulous. "What do you mean?"

He glanced down at the snakes as if they were nothing more than air. He said, "Never mind," waving his hand at them dismissively, and asked me again what I was doing.

"What do you mean? Don't you see the snakes?" I yelled, impatient and overwhelmed.

"Get down here," he said.

"Don't you see the snakes!" I said, desperation creeping into my voice.

"Just get down here," my father calmly insisted.

I had always trusted my father and never doubted that he had only my best interest at heart. Somehow I managed to defeat my terror long enough to climb down from the rock.

"See those snakes?" he said, pointing at them. "They can't touch you. You just do what you've got to do—don't worry about them."

In my dream his words had a calming effect but I can't say that in the moment my brain fully understood my father's message.

"They can't touch you," he said reassuringly.

Those words gave me strength. Maybe the snakes represented all the things I had been worried about—my lack of experience, my difficulty with English, money or other things I didn't even understand.

For my heart, it was a pivotal moment. I had been wallowing in fear and negativity, and it threatened to hold me back. But seeing my father again, even if it was just in a dream, was a powerful elixir. Like sunshine to a plant, my father's love and wisdom were nourishing. It was as if God was giving me a gift, or a helping hand.

I allowed my father's message to wash over me, to sustain me, and when I woke up, my debilitating anxiety had lessened. I felt like I could take those first few steps toward becoming a builder.

It was a learning experience all the way through. I did as much of the work myself as I could, including some of my own plumbing and my own wiring and electric work. I thought it would be easier and that I would save a lot of money that way, but it was slow-going. I'll never forget when the electrical inspector came to look at the house. He seemed like a nice man who didn't want to offend me—but then he insisted that I had to tear out all the improperly done wiring. Of course, it was the electrical work I had tried to do myself! But that inspector didn't just tell me what I was doing wrong. He showed me how to fix it too.

It took me six months just to learn how to do the wiring correctly. I remember staying up at night in our bedroom, trying to learn how to do it. The most difficult task I had was a light with two or three switches on it, and it was such a struggle to figure it out, I blew the fuses out in my own house many times.

At another point in the project, my father once again provided a helping hand. We had been pouring concrete at that time, and the mix had set too quickly, making it difficult to work with. I told the guys to forget it, that we would make a new batch and redo the job. But then I had another dream.

What I remember most about that dream was my father talking to me—scolding me, even.

"What do you mean you can't keep up?" he told me. "You go and roll up your sleeves and get up there and do that job."

I was a bit taken aback. After all, my father had been a farmer; he'd never worked in construction. Who was he to lecture me on such details, even if it was just a dream?

"Papa, what do you know about concrete?" I said gently. "I'm the one who has got to do the job."

"Did I ever tell you something that wasn't true?" he said, getting angry. "Are you questioning me?"

Suddenly I felt like I was four years old again and had just stolen matches from the kitchen. I was ashamed and embarrassed. But then I came to realize that while my father may have seemed angry in the dream, his visit was really another way of reassuring me and giving me confidence. It was a way to reinforce the idea that I shouldn't worry about what anyone else thought, and should just focus on my own goals and plans.

We went back and did the job with the hard-to-use concrete. I was now determined to make it work. And as it turned out, we did a beautiful job.

My father wasn't the only one who would visit me in my dreams. I do not remember much of this particular dream, but I do remember dreaming of my grandfather.

Seeing him with my unconscious mind, I knew that he was dead and remembered that my father was dead as well. I do not recall what my grandfather's message was, but I knew that he had come to tell me something important.

"Why did you come? Why not Papa?" I asked him.

"Oh, he comes for the big things, He sends me for the smaller things," my grandfather said with a wink.

It was just the sort of humor he had used all my life to educate and protect me. I remember waking up and feeling quite impressed.

I had spent $10,000 building this house and things were moving along, but I needed $5,000 to finish. During the project we were still able to save a little money, but not all that we needed and I knew there was a chance that I wasn't going to be able to get it from the bank.

Then there was another miracle. I felt like my father had been walking by my side during the whole project and then, when I needed it most, I knew that God was there for me too.

It wasn't always smooth sailing. There was a project being built next to mine and I knew the contractor who was handling the job. He and I were acquaintances and he had been a subcontractor who had worked on the framing for the first house I'd built. He asked what I was doing with myself. I told him that I was building another house.

"To live in?" he asked.

"No, to sell," I said.

"What do you mean?" he asked, getting angry. "You have a good job in a factory. You're taking up a job that could go to somebody else."

I was surprised by the man's anger, but I was undeterred. I always worked hard and yes, I almost always had more than one job, but I wasn't keeping anyone else out of a job. Perhaps he just resented having competition for construction work, but that's OK. There's nothing wrong with competition.

A few days later I got a phone call that initially scared me. At that time it was still pretty difficult for me to communicate in English. The man who called was one of the biggest builders in the county, and I was speechless. I couldn't think of what he would want from me.

I got a little nervous and, remembering how my friend had gotten so angry about my working while trying to build houses, I started thinking all kinds of crazy things. I thought the builder was trying to intimidate or scare me, and that he was calling to take my jobs away from me or something.

"David, are you there?" he said.

"Yes," I answered.

Then he asked me if I wanted to join the National Association of Home Builders. It wasn't exactly what I was expecting him to say.

"But can I be considered a builder?" I asked anxiously, remembering the issues I was having at the bank.

"Sure you are," he said. As it turned out, he had been doing his research, and knew a lot about me and my work.

He was a nice guy and a good man, and the way he treated me with such respect made me feel good. I said "yes" and joined the association, and that man became one of my good friends.

The construction of the second house went on and just at the point where we had the roof on the house and were doing the interior work, we had a stroke of luck. Someone made an offer to buy the house I was building and offered $2,500 as a down payment, which they gave directly to me.

Finally, there were no more roadblocks, no more problems. I didn't need anything from anybody and no one was standing in my way. It was the best feeling in the world. I was able to finish the house and sell it, making more money on that one job than I did in a year working at the factory. All my dreams became a reality—I was a builder.

We sold that house, a split entry, in 1970 for

$21,000—exactly the price I had been asking for. It was enough for us to pay all of the debts from the project and still have money left over.

That was enough to satisfy the requirements of the bank. In their eyes, I could now be called a builder, and they could work with me without any problems.

It was then that my mother, Marietta, agreed to come for a visit. I was overjoyed and made all the arrangements for her trip with a travel agency, to take advantage of a special travel deal they were offering. It was a long journey, especially for an older woman who didn't speak any English. We went to meet her at the airport, and I remember seeing her walk down the hallway toward us—and they had to stop me from running to her and giving her a hug.

"That's my mother, and I haven't seen her in nine years," I said to the man who stopped me from running to her.

He relented and let me go. I ran up and gave her such a hug! But she was very tired. I took her arm, carried her bags and helped her walk the rest of the way.

It was a pleasure having my mother there, seeing her meet my own children and showing her the home I had built for my family, and the second house I had just completed. I think it gave her a measure of comfort to see for herself that I really was doing OK. And by this time, I was knee-deep in work again, since I'd used some of the money from the sale of that house to purchase another lot.

I was in the midst of constructing an apartment building with four units, partially because I'd decided that being a landlord would be a good way to bring in some extra income. My mother would watch our kids, allowing Maria to come down and help me while I worked. Seeing her bond with the children was precious.

David was just a young toddler then, and my mother would speak to him in Italian and play with him. She would teach him all the names of the toys in Italian, and he loved it. They would play together and she'd be teaching him how to say "cow" and "horse" and "farm." He would only speak Italian with her, and it was amusing to watch because he would only speak to the rest of us in English!

I didn't want my mother to leave but the travel deal I'd made had a time limit, and if I was going to be able to pay a special rate she had to leave by a certain time. While we had been successful in selling that house, we still had to watch every penny to get by. By the time she decided to make the trip, there were just forty-five days—less than two months—for her to return under the restrictions of the travel agency's offer. We thought she would only want to stay for a couple of weeks, a relatively quick visit, so we never even mentioned the time limitation to her. But as the end of the forty-five days approached, she didn't seem to want to leave and I couldn't bring myself to make her go. I didn't even want to talk to her about it.

Maria didn't want to talk to her about it either. Neither of us had the guts to bring it up. I didn't know what to do, but finally Maria just looked at me and said, "Let's not worry about it."

Life went on. My mother stayed for eleven months; I even had to go to the consulate at one point and renew her visa. And in that time, God rewarded me and my family.

I was able to finish the four-unit apartment building but instead of keeping it, I wound up selling it for around $42,000. A friend of mine from the factory, his name was Joe, ended up buying it. He was always helping me out at work, translating for me when I had to talk to the bosses. He put $2,000 down to buy the building and signed the agreement on a Friday night after work.

I kept the check over the weekend because the banks were closed. Maria was supposed to bring the check to the bank on Monday morning, and I thought everything was fine, but then I saw Joe. He looked tormented. I realized that he was worried about the deal. It seemed like he was getting cold feet, and he was my friend, so I called Maria during the first coffee break and asked her if she had gotten to the bank yet.

She said "no," and I told her not to cash the check.

The entire week, Joe looked lost. By Thursday afternoon, I approached him and asked how he was doing.

"I'm a man of my word," he said a bit unsteadily.

I could see how upset he was, how worried, and I didn't want to see him like that anymore. No real estate deal was worth seeing my friend suffer like that.

"Tomorrow morning, bring back the agreement I gave you," I told him. "And I'll bring you the check back."

I could see the weight lift from his shoulders, and he lightened up considerably.

"Do you really want to do that?"

I said, "Sure." Everything seemed OK, but at quitting time Joe came back to talk to me.

He said that he appreciated the offer, but he was going to go through with our original agreement. And he did, and I could see the change in him—he went from looking and acting like a weakling to strutting around like a peacock. It was his first deal in real estate.

While that project had gotten underway, I had purchased another piece of land and begun a six-unit apartment building, and before it was even finished, someone had agreed to buy that building. All this, and I was still holding down my job at the factory.

What had started off as a struggle turned into an avalanche of success. I had no more problems with the bank, and we had an extra $40,000 in our pockets.

It was the summer of 1971, and my mother decided

she wanted to go home. Before, I had been so worried about the cost of bringing my family, all six of us, to Italy, but now I didn't even give it a second thought.

I bought tickets for her, myself, Maria and the kids, got permission for extra time off from the factory, and put $5,000 in my pocket—and took my whole family home to Italy.

The trip was wonderful. The funniest thing of all was that little David, who still would only speak Italian to my mother and English to everyone else, did not realize that everyone else in Italy spoke his grandma's special language too!

When I made that trip home, somehow everything looked smaller—even the mountain. We got reacquainted with the area and took the kids to see the Coliseum. It was a very special time.

Chapter Six

It was a beautiful time in my life. Selling the house and then the apartment buildings, with Maria by my side and my mother there to see it happen—this was the kind of success I had been striving for.

I was well on my way to achieving my dream. But that didn't mean that I stopped working hard or working at all my different jobs. In fact, even though I had made good money on the first house I'd sold, I always kept working at the factory and would still do construction work on the side when I could.

Some of that work was for my father-in-law. We lived close by, and Maria's parents adored our kids; her brothers and sisters were also nearby. But there was always a feeling that something wasn't quite right, an undercurrent of negative feeling, an unspoken attitude that I could only sometimes sense and didn't usually focus on.

Just as nature is cyclical, with patterns of life and death, growth and stormy destruction, playing themselves out over and over again, so is life. I knew that working hard and serving God were the ways in which I could achieve my own success, but that didn't mean that I was immune to problems. I had made my promise to God and to my father, but not everything was within my control. And though I had been shown so many times that I shouldn't worry about what other people thought, or about their bad intentions or jealousies, sometimes it wasn't easy. Sometimes, people didn't give me a choice.

When Maria and the kids and I had gotten back from our trip to Italy, the real estate market had slowed somewhat. It was hard to purchase lots, so in the meantime I picked up construction work where I could. It was then that Franco asked me to create an apartment above his garage for his daughter Gloria.

She was an attractive woman, but her life was not exactly on track—she lacked a lot of common sense and consideration for others. Though she was still in her twenties, she had been in a bad marriage, had two young children and gotten divorced, and was moving back in with her parents. I was happy to help Franco, though, and agreed without reservation.

He paid for the materials while I did the work for free, often in the evenings after I finished my shift at the factory. One day I was there working alone, drilling holes in the wall, when Gloria, who had been living in her parents' home while the apartment was being built, came in.

I looked up from my work and there she was, wearing a bikini. Gloria approached me and started coming on to me.

I didn't know what to think but my reaction was pretty quick.

"Gloria, you go downstairs and put some clothes on," I said, dismissing her.

She didn't listen. She continued to try to get my attention and touch me. I brushed her off and told her to go back downstairs, to get dressed.

Gloria apologized sheepishly, saying, "I'm sorry, I'm sorry," and left the room.

I went back to my work. I don't think it really dawned on me what Gloria was trying to do. I just focused on the construction. I thought the whole episode was over—but it wasn't.

The door slowly opened, and there she was again. This time, when Gloria came back into the room where I was working, she had just put on a tiny robe, buttoned in the front. She tried again to get my attention, to get in my way—to be provocative.

I got frustrated but I didn't say anything. I tried my best to ignore her and somehow, after a while, she got the hint and left.

So much of my life had been work, and then my wife and kids and building homes. I never spent a lot of time hanging around with the guys or in bars, or even away from my family. I never wanted to. If I wasn't working, there was no other place that I wanted to be than with my wife and children.

Nothing like this had ever happened to me before.

Even though I had now turned her down twice, Gloria came back again. I don't know why she thought I would do what she wanted. In her latest attempt, she was wearing an outfit that was worse than the ones before.

I was thirty-five years old. I had never had temptation like that before. But I believe that God was with me that night. There was a force in me that took over for a few moments as I looked at Gloria trying to entice me.

I gathered up my tools and left.

I walked to my truck, opened the door and got in the driver's seat. And then the true impact of what had happened became clear.

I could have kicked myself! I was overwhelmed with feelings of lust and regret and I couldn't believe what I had done. If you had told me beforehand that something like that was going to happen to me, that a beautiful woman would have given me a chance like that or been interested in me that way, I would not have believed it.

What the hell is wrong with me? I thought. *Where the hell am I going to get another opportunity like that?*

Those feelings swarmed inside of me, clouding my vision and making me feel like something had hit me over the head. I was out of sorts, full of sexual desire and the searing pain of feeling like a fool who passes on a sure thing. I wasn't myself.

Then I looked up from my inner confusion and saw something in the night sky, something far off. It was a small, bright circle but it wasn't a star. I didn't know what it was and had never seen anything like it with my waking eyes.

In a flash, the small circle seemed to be moving, and moving fast, toward me. It zoomed up to my face—and there before me was the image of my father.

It had been fifteen years or so since my beloved father had died in Italy. I had often thought of him, remembered him and even dreamed of him. But this was different.

I was wide awakc, conscious, and seeing him before me. The love, respect and admiration he'd always inspired in me rose to the surface, pushing aside the emotional conflict that had, just a few moments before, embroiled me. But what happened next stung me and changed my life.

Whatever this was—this vision, this image, or maybe even my father's spirit—fixed me with an intense stare. He looked angry and his eyes were like lasers aimed at mine.

"Is this the best you can do?" he demanded. "Is this the best you can do?"

Confusion overtook me. I didn't know what to say or do. My feelings were out of control, like a rollercoaster that trumped all my other thinking. In such a short time I had bounced from surprise at Gloria's actions to lust and regret, and then to bewilderment and joy at seeing my father. And then I realized what my father was saying.

I had made a promise.

I had pledged to God, and to my father and his memory and everything he represented, to live a life that served the Lord, to live a life of faith. I had told God that I would do the best I could do in my life.

And even though I had spent my life working so hard, struggling, keeping my faith in my hard work and my wife and family and truly enjoying the fruits of my labor, there I was feeling lust for another woman. Feeling regret because I had passed on an "opportunity" that not only would have ruined everything I'd ever wanted, but that would have hurt my precious, beloved wife and ripped my family apart.

My head and heart were reeling. My father's image seemed to just move away until it vanished. I had come so close to making a horrible mistake, to throwing away everything I had built. Then there was only one feeling that pushed out all the others, that marched through my soul like a tidal wave.

Shame.

The tears poured down my face. I was unable to stop crying. I had such shame in my heart, it was making me sick. I didn't know what to do or where to go.

I drove around for a while, thinking about what had happened and how stupid I was to have almost thrown it all away. My father's words and piercing tone of voice rang over and over in my ears: "Is this the best you can do? Is this the best you can do?"

As I thought and drove, I came to realize that God was by my side that night, and how much power he had exerted in the evening's events. It was with the help of God that I was able to walk away from Gloria's temptations. It was God who had sent this vision of my father to remind me of the promise I'd made when I was just twenty years old, of the path I had chosen so long ago to walk.

I had always been very proud of myself, but when I had left the apartment I had been taken over by arrogance. It is the only way to explain how the lust and regret had been so powerful within me. My father's mystical visit had rescued me. The fact that this had been no dream, that I'd truly seen him before my eyes, only speaks to God's power.

When my father scolded me, it transformed that arrogance to a weeping, deep humility. I felt like a big coward.

My father and God were the two things I would not, could not betray. My father's appearance was all at once a reminder, a warning and a helping hand, and I took it seriously. I felt that my father had become one of God's troops, one of a fleet of angels God has sent to me in my life.

With my swollen eyes and tear-stained cheeks, I knew I couldn't go straight home. I drove around for a while, thinking about everything, and knew deep down that this time I was lucky, that God had given me a chance to continue to live my life in his service. But I also decided that I couldn't be sure that Gloria wouldn't bother me again. I wasn't sure I would be strong enough to resist again, since I was so unfamiliar with that kind of temptation.

There was only one thing to do. I had to embrace the truth no matter what. It was the only way I could reaffirm my promise to God, to honor all that my father meant to me and the importance of the life I had built with Maria.

I didn't know how to tell Maria, though. How do you tell your wife something like that? I was also afraid. I had always believed in God but never in my wildest dreams had I believed that spirits actually existed. Seeing my father's image so tangibly had been startling, and it had unsettled me. I was a bit lost, but I knew there was no other choice and when I got home, I prepared myself for the worst.

I do not think Maria ever looked at my face; she did not seem to realize that I had been upset, that I had been crying. She was setting the table for dinner and talking a bit but I was not really engaged in the conversation. I knew I couldn't wait to talk to her about this; I knew I had to tell her. But it was like a lump in my throat and at first I couldn't get the words out. Finally, I took a deep breath and spoke.

"Maria," I said solemnly and carefully. "You better come to work with me when I go down there."

"Why?" she said, turning around.

Somehow, she understood right away what I was getting at. She looked at my face, really looked, and knew something had happened.

"Your sister doesn't act too nicely with me," I said, still measuring my words.

Maria got upset, but not in the way I'd thought she would. I wasn't prepared for what happened next.

"You better treat her nice," she said angrily. "You better not touch her."

She refused to come with me to work.

I couldn't even speak. I was stunned. She didn't believe me. In fact, she seemed to believe the worst of me.

I was at a terrible loss. I couldn't understand really what was going on, why Maria would react like that, why all of this was happening. I was on my own in dealing with the situation, and for a few moments I didn't know what to do. Then I realized that I had to just do my best, to stay strong and resist the temptation as much as I could.

The next day I went back to Franco's garage, to keep working on the apartment. I hesitated but knew that I had no choice, since I couldn't go back on my promise to my father-in-law. I started to work and was almost afraid that Gloria would appear, trying to distract me again.

Then I looked out the window and there she was, in a bikini and looking like a Victoria's Secret model while she set up a lawn chair in the grass right under the window where I was working. I tried my best not to look, and I don't think she knew that I was looking, but it was hard to keep my eyes off of her because she was making such a spectacle of herself. I was feeling strong in my resolve to be faithful, though, and Gloria's efforts weren't bothering me or affecting me as much as they had the night before.

Suddenly, Maria drove up, pulling the car into the driveway like a bullet. She got out and took three steps forward, and then stopped. Maria seemed frozen for a moment, taking in the scene of what her sister was doing before she turned around and left.

As soon as Gloria had seen Maria, she composed herself a bit. And I felt better, stronger. The temptation lessened until there was none, and I could see the situation for what it was. I knew that I had made the right choice by not giving in.

When I finished work that day and went home to Maria, I hoped things would be different. I came into the house.

"Maria, do you see what I mean?" I said quietly.

"Yes," she said, and it appeared that she was still a bit taken aback by what she had seen. "Yes, because if it was you who was bothering her, she would not have been out there like that."

Now Maria knew the truth, really knew it for herself. And after that situation, nothing Gloria did could bother me. But sadly, she tried several more times after that. Gloria would attempt to tease me and act provocatively, wearing inappropriate outfits and striking poses that were probably meant to tempt me. But it didn't work. Where I had once been shocked and afraid of what I would do if tempted again, I was now solid in my faith and belief that God was with me, and nothing could break that.

Looking back, I believe that it was simply a war for my heart and mind that the Devil didn't want to lose, and so he used Gloria to try to get at me, to win me from the arms of God. And it seemed so easy for evil to regroup, to keep coming after me. That's the only explanation I had for her repeated efforts and inappropriate behavior. But I prayed and kept my faith where it had always been, and just worked as I always had to serve God. I knew that He wouldn't let me down.

It was as if I had gone through the fire and now couldn't be burned. I had gone through that lesson with the help of God and my father, and even though it was more than fifteen years after he'd died, I feel like that was when I became a real man.

At that point, I thought that the situation had resolved itself. I thought that the horrible moments were done and out of my life. Little did I know what was about to come next.

We must all plant and nurture and tend to the good in ourselves, our lives and this world. We need to nourish our faith and help it grow the same as a carefully planned garden needs love and affection to reach its full potential. But it is not only the good things in life that can be planted or grown.

Just as easily as people can sow seeds of love, of generosity and kindness, so too can evil find its way into our lives. Sometimes it only takes a small seed of doubt, or a tiny deception, to undermine our more positive endeavors.

I thought that the situation with Gloria was finished, that it stayed between her, myself and Maria and was no longer a threat. I was wrong.

When Gloria realized that she couldn't influence me

and couldn't control me, she seemed to want revenge. It appeared that she wanted to make me pay, to make me suffer, for rejecting her advances.

So, she started to spread rumors about me. She even told my daughter.

And though Maria had seen the truth with her own eyes, and knew for herself that it was Gloria at fault and I had done nothing wrong, something changed. She heard the rumors, of course—I don't think Gloria knew that I had told Maria anything—and those rumors started to eat away at my wife's faith. She started to doubt me.

I remember one night, right after all this had happened, when Gabriella was seven or eight years old and she and I were out in the driveway together, talking, when Franco pulled up, parking his car next to the driveway.

"Nonno's coming," Gabriella said, and she seemed just a little bit nervous. Even she felt the tension that had sprung up because of Gloria's lies.

I was nervous too. I thought that maybe Franco had heard the lies, and thought I was doing something with Gloria, and had come to defend his daughter. I steadied myself, trying to be ready for whatever would happen, and was feeling defensive. But then Franco just said, "Hello," putting his hands on Gabriella's head as he walked by, asking her, "How are you doing?" before heading into the house.

I didn't know what to think. I found out later that he went inside and went upstairs to talk to Maria, but he only really had one thing to say.

"Don't believe one word that Gloria said," he told her.

He only stayed a few minutes before he left again. But Franco was a man of honor. He loved his kids, he loved his family, but by this time he had worked with me and seen the kind of man I was. He knew I wouldn't hurt Maria or betray my family and he came to tell Maria that.

Sometime earlier, I had taken a trip to Italy to attend the wedding of one of my nephews. A friend of ours at the time had asked me to buy jewelry for her while I was there, a gold chain and cross. She wanted to give it to someone as a present, and I didn't think anything of it at the time. I brought it back for her and she was grateful.

One day, my mother-in-law was at the bank and overheard some of the tellers talking. One of them was showing off a gold chain. My mother-in-law heard the woman talk about how a contractor friend of hers had just brought it back from Italy, just for her.

Right away, my mother-in-law got it in her head that I was that contractor—and that this woman in the bank must have been my girlfriend or something. Of course, she told Maria as soon as she could, saying,

"That pig of a husband of yours has a girlfriend!" and telling her the story.

At first, Maria was upset and gave me quite a hard time when I got home. But I started laughing as soon as I realized what had happened, and reminded her about the gold chain I had brought back for that friend. Then Maria relaxed too, but it showed how right away, my mother-in-law was suspicious of me.

Then, one day, my mother-in-law came over and starting having an argument with Maria. She was quite angry and made it clear to Maria that she was not happy. My mother-in-law seemed intent on taking her anger at the situation out on Maria and me, and it was something I just couldn't understand. I just don't know what the point was—if she really wanted Maria and me to split up, or if there was anything for them to gain from us doing so. Maybe I should have taken my mother-in-law's anger as a sign and been able to realize that the situation with Gloria was not finished, as I had thought it was. But I was trusting that the situation had been taken care of, and was done.

After a few weeks things seemed to subside, and it felt like everything was getting back to normal. Life appeared to get back on track and the shame I felt at my weakness lessened; the pain the episode had caused looked like it had passed.

I thought things were OK and I went about my

life as I always had, working my two or three jobs and spending my rare free time with Maria and the kids, who were all growing up healthy and strong. But little did I know that the deception and lies continued. This was going on all around me, but I didn't know it. My family had been poisoned and there was a lack of faith growing alongside all of the good, positive things I was trying to plant, taking root and changing the course of my family's life without my even knowing it.

But I have come to realize that a life spent serving God is not without its difficulties. Just because I was working toward my own goals in a way that honored God's love and faith did not mean that I would get a free pass from life's troubles.

Certainly, I had not had an easy life—a childhood spent surrounded by bloody war, growing up working hard on my family's farm, not being able to finish school, my father's death and now, the problems caused by my sister-in-law. These were all obstacles to the pure life I was trying to live.

When I say "pure," I do not mean without fault. Faults and troubles are part of what make us human. But it is how we overcome those difficulties that sets us apart, that distinguishes us. There is a Bible verse that speaks to this: "My son, when you come to serve the Lord prepare yourself for a trial."

I believe that God walks with us always. I believe—my faith tells me—that the Devil is always nearby as well, just waiting for an opportunity to tempt us off of our paths. When there is a battle, it is the Devil who often flees while God stays strong beside us. Gloria's temptations were like a secret pit prepared for me, something for me to fall into when I wasn't looking so that those few seconds of lust would lead to me being snared by evil.

It was not just the promises I had made to God, to my father and to myself that saved me in those days. There was another lesson in all of this, one I've learned over and over again in my life, whether it was because I had stolen matches or was trying to cheat in a bicycle race. The truth is so powerful, and like God it can do so much to help people. But the truth is not about getting people to believe what you say or making yourself feel better when you have done something wrong. That is shallow, selfish behavior.

The truth is about what really is true. And what really counted for me was my family, my beautiful Maria, my wonderful kids and my faith. They were like a light shining just to inspire me. The light of love and of family, of human kindness, is something almost everyone carries within themselves and after this trial, I was determined to make that light shine brightly and hold it up for all to see.

Months later, there was a night on which, once again, God showed me that he was always by my side. Each night, while I lay in bed next to Maria, I used to bless my kids, saying a little prayer for each of them in my mind, asking God to watch over them and take care of them.

But one night as I did this, I heard something strange coming from Gabriella's room. She did not sound right. In fact, she seemed to be whining or whimpering in her sleep, which was quite unusual. At first I just thought maybe she was having some sort of indigestion, had eaten something too heavy, and that it was bothering her. I tried not to give it too much thought.

The next night, though, it happened again, and I knew that something was wrong, that she was being tormented in some way. Inside of my mind and soul, I fiercely screamed, "Go away!" It was as if I were shouting at the evil that seemed so present. I don't know exactly what was going on, but I felt as though I had to do something and that was all that was within my power to do.

Then Gabriella gave a high-pitched scream. I leapt out of bed with a strong feeling that something was wrong. What was strange was that Maria, a very light sleeper, didn't wake up when Gabriella yelled out.

I went to check Gabriella and felt her forehead for a fever or signs of illness, but her head was cool to the touch and she didn't seem to be sick. I checked on Paula and went to the boys' room, looking in on Lorenzo and David, making sure they were under their blankets. Everything seemed alright. I couldn't see anything wrong.

I didn't need to see something wrong to know that something was wrong. It was like there was a darkness that I could feel in the fiber of my being. I went through the whole house, looking and checking, and then, I prayed. I asked God to shield my family and my house from whatever that dark presence was, to shield and protect my kids from that. I never said anything to my wife or anyone else about what had happened; I didn't want them to be afraid or think there was something wrong with the house. The next night everything was fine.

I waited a while, but eventually, about a year or two later, I told Maria what had happened. I thought she might find it strange, but the only thing she said was, "Why didn't you tell me?"

Years later, after Gabriella was married, I brought up that night when she was just about eleven years old. She said that about that time, when she was attending Catholic school, it had been miserable. Every day she would go cry in the bathroom; she'd had a hard time making friends and was very unhappy. But one day, all the bad feelings she'd been having, the tough times, had just stopped. School hadn't been so horrible anymore, and she had made friends.

"Papa, it must have been about that time," she said.

As time went on the real estate market picked back up. I was getting more and more work as a builder but ran into some problems. I didn't really face discrimination, but because of the language barrier and, I think, my lack of education, I had a hard time getting contracts the traditional way. So, I changed my strategy. I stopped trying to put in offers for jobs and instead concentrated on buying properties.

I would purchase the lots and then advertise them. When someone came along and wanted to buy the lot for a new home, I then got the job to build that home. It was a trick that worked and allowed me to build not only my business but my reputation.

Sometimes, people would come around and say that they had their own builder, but when that happened, I just told them to get their own lot!

At first my strategy made Maria nervous. When I started buying up lots she was terrified. But when things started going well, it was Maria who was scouring the newspaper, looking for lots to buy.

I would buy lots here and there, but I also was able to purchase a portion of a larger farm, the first such land deal I did, which was about 120 acres. I had approached the owner about a year earlier but she had declined to sell me any land, saying that she'd felt as though she had to sell the whole thing all at once.

A year later she changed her mind and gave me a call.

"I'll take you up on your offer," the owner said, selling me fourteen acres at $2,500 each.

I ended up getting forty-two lots out of that land and did quite well. In fact, it seemed like each project was getting easier and more profitable.

I was getting a good reputation, and more success along with it. At this stage I was also focusing on building apartment buildings and made more money with every job, though I wanted to keep some of those buildings for myself at some point, to be able to collect rental income. I never stopped building houses, though, getting three or four such projects done each year.

There was one deal I won't soon forget. It was a young couple who wanted to buy a house from me, and they had put down a $5,000 down payment. But there was a time period of about forty-five to sixty days before the deal was final and in the meantime, they discovered they were going to have a baby.

That was when they wanted out of the deal, but they thought that they would lose their down payment because that was what it said in the agreement. They approached me cautiously and explained what had happened before asking for half of their down payment back. I told them it wasn't a problem and gave them a check for the whole $5,000.

They were stunned, and they insisted I keep something for my time and expense but I told them "no," that God would like it better this way.

For me, it was simply a question of following what God would have wanted me to do. It wasn't a question of money or what would have been best for me. Living in the pleasure of God is not about getting everything you want or treating God as if he were some kind of magic genie, there to grant your wishes and nothing more. It is more about doing the right thing and doing it with honor and integrity, about praying to God and keeping your heart and mind open to his greater desires. I could have kept that young couple's money, but what good would it have done? They needed it more.

It was just like a few years before that, when my friend Joe had been getting cold feet about our first real estate deal. I could have gone ahead and cashed his check without any regard for his feelings or anxiety. But what kind of man would that have made me? I don't know, and I don't want to know. It was more important to me that my friend be comfortable with the deal, that he not suffer because of an agreement we made.

It was the same in every aspect of my business. I never skimped on the materials I used for building houses. I would rather have used materials that cost a little bit more money so that I could put out a quality product even if it meant that I'd have less profit at the end of the day. Truly, money isn't everything.

For me, it was about more than just my bottom line. I conducted my business the way I have always tried to conduct my life, and while I always worked hard I didn't want to forsake my humanity along the way. I have found that it is a philosophy, a way of living and working, that has brought me more success than I ever could have imagined.

I steadily built and sold apartment buildings as the 1970s crept on, in the end selling about half of what I'd built and keeping the rental income. The small development I had begun at that farm did well and by 1975 I had already purchased a large backhoe to make the work easier.

I had a good relationship with the bank in those days. It cost about $60,000 to build a six-unit apartment building in those days, and I would never borrow more than $100,000 at once. But when a certain piece of property caught my attention, I started to dream a little bigger, to set my sights a bit higher. That lot was a bit large and I figured it was out of my league, but then I went to the bank.

I talked to the manager at the bank, the same man who had once told me that I couldn't borrow any money because I wasn't a builder.

"I want to ask you a question," I said, "but I don't think you'll go for it."

"What?" he said.

"I want to build twenty-four units," I said. "What is the limit I can borrow?"

"Well, bring me the plans and bring me the project and we'll talk," he said.

The property I had been looking at was a commercial lot, and the original buyer had lost the property when he'd neglected to pay the taxes on it. The city had taken the land back.

The banker said that he wanted to take a look at the property.

We went by the lot. The banker looked around and seemed to approve, and it was as if he saw the same potential in the property that I did.

"There's a shop right there, and a bus stop right here," he said. "The old people would love to live here."

"So what's my limit? How much can I borrow?" I asked.

"You bring us the right project," he said, "and there is no limit."

It was a vote of confidence I had never gotten before, and one I wanted to take full advantage of. I took a leap of faith and decided it was time to dedicate myself full-time to this career. In January 1976, I quit my job at the factory. After thirteen years with the company, I was giving up a certain amount of job security and my benefits, but it was a move I had to make. I ended up borrowing $220,000 and started work that fall on the twenty-four-unit apartment building.

The place ended up costing me $260,000 to build and as soon as I was done a real estate man offered me $480,000 for it, but I didn't sell. A few years earlier, I had sold a few dozen units and regretted doing so.

I kept the twenty-four-unit building for decades. I had taken a risk when I'd quit my job at the factory but it paid off in more ways than one, as my net worth expanded considerably: All told, I had almost $1 million to my name.

Chapter Seven

I had achieved a level of material wealth I had never known before, and it felt like all the hard work Maria and I had done had finally paid off. I had a good reputation as a builder; we had our home and four beautiful children.

And oh, how those kids had grown up. Gabriella was eighteen years old and studying to become a real estate agent. At fourteen, Paula was just becoming a teenager. And David, the baby of the family, was already ten.

Then there was Lorenzo. Our boy, who as a tiny infant had been so sick and so helpless, had grown up quite a bit. By the time he was fifteen years old he was six feet tall and was a one of the best football players at the junior varsity level. He had a great personality and everyone liked him.

One day a very nice man called the house and told us that he wanted to come over and discuss Lorenzo's future. I don't remember too much about the man, though Maria had insisted he was a priest. I was a man of God, but that didn't matter to me; my reaction to his phone call was swift. I got pretty mad pretty quickly and didn't give the man a chance to say anything else.

"My son has a right to grow up and to make up his own mind," I said, and that was the end of it.

Looking back, I wonder now if there was something in the air, some sign that I was missing or a guardian angel trying to send me a signal that I just wouldn't see. I don't regret telling that man that Lorenzo could make up his own mind. I don't have any regrets at all. But it wasn't long before we needed all the angels we could get.

It was 1979, and Gabriella and I had both been taking classes at a local real estate office. She was going for her real estate license. I thought it would be great for her and that she would then be able to help me with paperwork. I was in the classes to further my education and understanding of the real estate business. Even after all of my success I still felt insecure about my fifth-grade education and kept trying to overcome it.

We were both in class one night when a police officer walked in and interrupted.

The officer called out my name, asking if I was there.

"That's me," I said slowly, not knowing what to do or say. "What's wrong?"

"Oh, well, you better call the hospital," the officer said.

I was able to use a nearby desk phone and got a nurse at the hospital. "Your son is in critical condition," the nurse said.

It was one of the strangest, most frightening moments of my life.

"Which one? Which son?" I asked, trying to understand what the nurse was saying and becoming more frantic with each moment.

The nurse said that she didn't know.

"Is he ten, or is he fifteen?" I asked.

The nurse said that it must have been the fifteen-year old, because he looked like a big kid.

My heart sunk, and I knew immediately that God had come calling for my son and this time, he would not give him back.

"Lorenzo is sick," I said to Gabriella, "and I'm sure this time God is not going to give him back to us."

It was a ten-mile drive to the hospital. There wasn't much traffic and in reality it probably took ten to fifteen minutes to make the trip—but it was the longest drive of my life.

It felt like there was a heavy stone on my chest. All I could think about was my son, what must have happened, and of his illness as an infant. The first time he'd been so gravely ill it had been a miracle recovery; he'd seemed to gain five pounds overnight and had been almost mysteriously restored to health.

This time, I knew there would be no miracle.

When we finally made it to the hospital and into Lorenzo's room, I knew. I touched him, and I knew it wasn't right. He was dead. He'd been dead when they'd called me.

My heart was broken that day. None of us were ever the same; I think it was years before I saw the joy come back to Maria's face. Our entire family, our lives, changed course that day.

We were devastated. David suffered so much, losing his big brother. He was a football player, just like Lorenzo, and had played baseball. He had been so strong through the whole ordeal. He was a great athlete, but I remember watching him play one day after Lorenzo's death and he just lost his focus. It was his turn to bat, but his mind was just somewhere else that day; the umpire ended up yelling, "Ball four!" three times before David realized what had happened. I could tell he was so hurt.

Gabriella and I quit real estate school. My wife changed overnight. Lorenzo's death seemed to instantly take ten years off her life. Our grief seemed overwhelming; our mourning was endless. The tears flowed freely and each of us would just cry out of the blue. Our lives, our attitudes, changed course. It was a terrible time.

And even then, throughout it all, the deception and pettiness of my brother-in-law and sister-in-law were working to hurt us, operating behind the scenes to unravel the little that was left of our lives.

It was the greatest loss of my life. My father's death had left an indelible mark and was something I never thought I would be able to get over. My family had struggled because of the loss, but he had been sick for a long time before his death. We'd known there was a chance that he wouldn't make it and though you'd never think it could happen, we'd been able to prepare a little bit.

But for a boy of fifteen who was so full of life and energy to just be gone…

I used to get mad at God for taking him. I would go to the cemetery nearly every day. I just wanted him to come back. The grief seeped into every part of my day, leaving me without a moment's peace. Even when I would go to lock the door at night, I almost didn't want to; even though I knew better, it just felt like I was locking Lorenzo out of the house. My hand felt heavy with dread and sorrow each time I had to put the lock in place.

It wasn't until later that I learned what had happened. It had been a typical day in every way: Lorenzo had mowed the lawn and gone for a run with his friends. He'd been at a friend's home a couple of blocks away, hanging out with his buddies, when he'd started wrestling with one of them. And then, without warning, he had collapsed.

The doctor that had performed the autopsy had discovered a problem with Lorenzo's heart. There was a defect we had never known was there, with the vein that brings blood to the heart, and when he'd died, it must have been instantly.

The doctors had marveled at Lorenzo's height and athletic shape. They couldn't believe he'd been an athlete, that he had never had chest pains or other problems. They couldn't believe he'd lived as long as he did. They'd thought it wasn't possible, given the problem with his heart.

Given Lorenzo's problems, ones we didn't even know he had, I guess it was a miracle that he had lived those fifteen years, a miracle that we got to be with him and know him and love him.

When people suffer and tragedy visits them, I often see that they get mad at God, just like I did. And that anger makes them grow further away from the church. I had always tried to live my life in the service of God and I was angry with him, but I couldn't help but think that there was something wrong with me, to think that I shouldn't question his will.

The more I thought about it, the longer I mourned. I came to understand that God had cured Lorenzo's illness when he was an infant, and had given him back to us. But after all those years, God couldn't spare him anymore.

I struggled for so long. In some ways I still do. You lose your grandfather, you lose your own father—but it's nothing like losing your young son.

But finally I reached a certain place in my heart where I could no longer question myself or God. I came to the conclusion that God had wanted to do something for Himself, and that He used us—myself and Maria—to do it. I can feel honored by that. And when you see all the things young people endure in their lives, all the pain, Lorenzo didn't have to go through any of that. In so many ways he got to enjoy just the best years of his life. He left before the pain of life really started, and I began to feel like he was maybe better off in heaven, by God's side.

It wasn't that the pain stopped. The loss of a child is an ache that never goes away. I was depressed, but in those days my spirituality, my faith in God, seemed to take over in a way I couldn't explain. Perhaps it was just a willingness to submit to God's will, to close my eyes and walk where He lead me instead of using anger and bitterness to resist. I was suffering, but I wasn't beaten down. Thinking about God actually made it easier to deal with. Losing Lorenzo was God's will and though it hurt unbelievably, I would never rebel against God.

Maria, though, was destroyed. She was a shell of herself—what mother wouldn't be? I had always tried to give her courage and I knew that I couldn't do that if I was beaten down myself.

Lorenzo died in late May 1979. One of my sisters,

one of my brothers and my cousin made the trip from Italy to America for his funeral. It was exactly two weeks after his death, just a few days before my relatives were due to go home. Maria was practically a zombie, and everything was somber. Life seemed dull and gray.

And while it seemed unthinkable, some people were just cruel. I always just focused on my own work, but others apparently didn't see it that way. People in the community apparently looked at me and thought all I cared about was money.

After Lorenzo died, some old man I didn't even know called me up. "How do you feel now, with all this money, and now your son's gone?" he said tauntingly.

I was stunned. I didn't even know the man and never knew that people felt that way. I didn't even know what to say.

Despite the grief, there was still work to be done. Everyone was at our house, and I had a van in those days. It was dinnertime and I had been digging a foundation for a new project. I was moving the van with my cousin and when we got into the driveway he started yelling, shouting in surprise.

There were two deer, beautiful young bucks, each with six-point antlers, in front of us. They bounced pass my excited cousin as if they didn't even see us and began an unlikely but beautiful dance in our backyard.

The lithe creatures seemed to move as if they were in slow motion, exchanging moves and jumping and playing with each other so gracefully it was as if they were putting on a show for us all.

They don't really have any deer in Italy and my brother, who was also with us, had never seen one. He was so excited he wanted to try to catch one and I had to put my hands up in front of him to keep him from running after one of the animals.

Maria, her father, Franco, and my sister were all in the kitchen when the deer appeared, and Maria had been crying, overwhelmed with the grief that had become her constant companion. There was a window in the kitchen looking out over the backyard, and when the deer came, my sister stood, amazed at the sight, but something even better than that happened. It was as if Mother Nature were giving us a little gift, something gentle and soothing to ease our pain, and the gift finally allowed Maria to find some peace.

We all stood, entranced by the dance and the motion and wishing it would go on but eventually, my brother couldn't resist the temptation anymore. He said, "Let's catch one!" and ran off after the bucks before I could stop him.

Later, when I looked at a calendar, I realized that the appearance of the deer was more than just a coincidence, and had arrived on a very special day: June 12, the anniversary of my father's death.

I missed both my son and my father so much, it was a grief that seemed to intertwine.

The visit from those powerful, supple animals wasn't the only time when I felt that my father was somehow taking care of Lorenzo on the other side.

As I had before in a crucial moment in my life, I had a dream about my father. This time, I dreamt of both Lorenzo and he wearing gorgeous, $2,000 suits and looking very classy as they were busy doing something together. I was watching them from far off; I don't know if they were paying any attention to me.

We were all in a garden along with my cousin from Piglio, the cousin who had married Maria and me and who was so loved throughout the town for his generosity and kindness. The garden was big and had a tall fence. As the images flicked through my unconscious mind I saw a group of people, including my son, my father and my cousin. But then my son seemed to grab my cousin by his robes and stop him for a minute.

"Hey, my father came to see me here—not you," Lorenzo told him.

I got closer and closer but woke up before I could hug or talk to Lorenzo in the dream. It was like feeling the grief all over again, but it was also more than that. There was a more positive idea to be had. That dream was like another message from my father, a message of comfort and hope that let me know that Lorenzo was alright, that my father was looking after him.

Around the time that Lorenzo died, I was reading in the Bible about Noah and the flood. As the story goes,

God invented the rainbow when he promised Noah he would never again send such a dreadful flood; the rainbow became a reminder to God to keep his promise. After reading about that, I grew a beard myself, and still wear one. In my own way, the beard is like a rainbow, a symbol to remind God that he already took one of my children, and not to take another one.

For the longest time I visited the cemetery regularly, stopping by Lorenzo's grave. I seemed compelled to make the visits and it became a kind of habit. It took many years but after a while something changed, a shift I couldn't really see or feel but one that happened nonetheless. Time worked its magic, and then I would drive by the cemetery but forget to stop. The visits became less frequent until finally, I didn't need to go all the time.

That was when I realized that I wasn't mourning anymore. I would take a drive through the cemetery and not even think about seeing his grave; I'd get to the other side and even a second time wouldn't remember. Time truly does heal, and eventually the pain subsides. Then you realize you are restored.

Chapter Eight

People, like plants, like nature, sometimes go dormant. We experience trouble, loss, difficulty, and it changes us. We can lose our spark, our bloom; instead of living with the vibrancy of God's light in our hearts, instead of using the good that surrounds us to produce a bright flower, we shrink a bit. Life gets darker and it's harder to do the things we love, the things we know we should do.

Just as a plant with a strong root system, a solid foundation, can survive a frost, so too can people. We are rocked by the problems in our lives: the loss of a child, the cruelty of other people. Yet if we remember our roots—faith in God, the love of family, a willingness to work hard—we can make it through the darkest times.

But sometimes just making it through is not enough. There are times in which we must plant seeds in our lives and nurture our futures as if we were tending to a garden—planning, watching, caring for the plants and protecting them against blight. Planting a garden is not only an exercise of faith, but an investment in Mother Nature.

Not everything that gets planted is good. Deception and grief can find places in the gardens of our lives, just as weeds can sprout up or animals can infiltrate and eat the leaves off the plants. We cannot possibly protect ourselves or our loved ones from every danger that might come along.

The rumors my sister-in-law spread about me had changed the course of my life, my family, without my even knowing it. My son's passing was like a tornado ripping its way through my life and family, destroying so much of what we knew. The loss of a child is the kind of grief that, while it may heal or fade, never completely goes away. With time, I felt restored but Lorenzo's death is like a wound on my heart that healed but left a scar. The scar never really goes away.

It is the good parts of ourselves, our lives—the foundations we build with help from our loved ones, the inner strength we develop through time, experience and the choices we make—that serve as protection against the bad things. But we cannot be passive, letting the good bolster us and the bad pummel us whenever chance brings them our way. We must plant good things in our gardens as well. It may take time to see the fruits of our labor but those fruits are all the sweeter for it.

I had been, in a way, planting seeds for my career as a builder for years: working hard and saving my money; changing my strategy when I couldn't bid for jobs the traditional way; earning a good reputation with every job; developing a relationship with the bank; and educating myself about American construction until finally, I was able to build that large, twenty-four-unit apartment building.

The harder I worked, and the more I put my faith in God and my father's message that I should focus on my own goals, the more it paid off. As the years went by my net worth expanded, my family became more secure and I was able set my sights even higher than I had in the past.

Around the same time that Lorenzo passed away, there was a farm for sale. It was 125 acres, a beautiful piece of land with gently rolling hills, and even though it was in a different town, it was adjacent to the other farm where I had previously purchased land.

The farm I was eyeing then was twenty minutes from the city, only a mile from the highway—the perfect place for a development. A millionaire had made an agreement to buy it but then had backed out before the deal was finalized, leaving it back in the hands of the original owners, who were four brothers.

In 1980, I had twenty lots to my name. But real estate was bad in those years; the interest rates at the bank were extremely high, the economy was tough and I was struggling. It was so difficult to sell property I almost couldn't give the land away.

Though times were difficult economically, I felt strongly that there was something more for me to achieve. It wasn't enough anymore for me simply to construct apartment buildings or houses one at a time. I had a larger vision in mind, something that would allow me to really put my skills and experience to work.

I had my eye on that farm and was thinking about the future, and so I made an offer to buy it. It was a coveted piece of property. I was talking to a surveyor just a month before I offered to buy the land.

"You want to buy that farm? Are you crazy?" the surveyor said. "Everybody wants to buy that farm."

But when the brothers heard that I could put up $75,000 as a down payment, they decided to do business with me. What I didn't know at the time was how much they were counting on me to fail—and that someone in my own family was gleefully watching from the sidelines to see it happen.

Maria's brother, Pasqualino, was good friends with those brothers. Pasqualino and Assunta had been living in this corner of Pennsylvania before I'd arrived in America, and they were known in the area as good people and were very well-liked.

But throughout the years Pasqualino had reserved a certain intimidating attitude just for me, treating me so badly in private that no one would have believed it. I had just endured his behavior, believing, as I always had, that it was more important to focus on my goals and dreams. I knew that if I paid no attention to the troubles around me, I couldn't really be hurt, just as my father had shown me how to ignore the hissing, slithering snakes in a dream.

So it was with that feeling that I was eyeing the purchase of the farm. It was a risk, but until that point I'd never had any real problems or hit an obstacle that I was not able to work my way through. When I had set my mind to doing something, I was usually able to do it. So, just as I had done throughout my life, I forged ahead with the faith that God would be by my side, and that all it would take was hard work for me to reach this goal.

The agreement I struck with those brothers called for me to pay off the farm in five years. The agreement had a provision that stated that if I could not finish making my payments, I would still walk away with any land I'd already paid for—but the brothers would keep my $75,000 down payment.

Around this time our children were starting to

grow up and become adults. Maria and I had always agreed—in fact, it was one of the first major decisions we'd made as parents—that we would give our kids the best educations possible. We'd paid for good schools for our kids throughout the years, and Gabriella, Paula and David all had gone to college. They didn't have a dime of student loans to pay when they graduated, either.

It was the best investment we could have made as parents and quite an achievement. After all, they were the children of Italian immigrants whose English was not so good when we'd arrived there. We couldn't exactly help them with their English or math homework. They did everything on their own, and Gabriella even accomplished four years of college in just three years.

After college, a wonderful thing happened. Gabriella, my oldest, got married.

It was a beautiful September day in 1982 when Gabriella married her longtime boyfriend, Paul. Gabriella had just finished college. When she'd started dating him she'd been just sixteen years old and she'd come home one night from a festival at church. Gabriella was always such a good Italian girl; she'd approached me out of the blue with a serious look on her face.

"Papa, I have to tell you something," she'd said.

"What?" I'd said.

"I was talking to a boy last night," she'd said solemnly.

"So what?" I'd said, confused.

As it turned out, she'd thought she wasn't allowed to talk to boys! I had never laid down rules like that, so I thought it was pretty funny. But Gabriella was always very respectful, very considerate of Maria and me—more so than I was at her age.

Watching Gabriella, along with my other children, get married was both a sad and wonderful experience. Paula got married to her husband, Patrick, just seven years later, and David met and married his wife, Terri, just a few years after that.

There are so many mixed emotions when watching your children get married. There is happiness because they are happy, and at the same time it is a complicated, fearful and somewhat sad time for a parent as you wonder what is going to happen to your kids as they embark on their new life's journey. You wonder if they will be alright. You think about what kind of people your kids are marrying, if they will be taken care of. Those are the kinds of questions every parent has, but ones that can only be answered by time.

In my case, time has brought a very pleasant result as all the people my children married have only ended up growing our family and adding to our happiness.

In the early 1980s I decided it was time to use some of my success to help my own family, and we decided to build ourselves a bigger home. We loved our first house, a ranch with its fireplaces and porch, but I was looking for something a bit more spacious.

As time went on I had been allowed to buy more and more of that farm until I held another thirty-three acres. I chose a piece of that land and in 1984 built a new split-level with a fruit cellar under the patio. Even though we only moved 300 or 400 yards away from the ranch, it was like a different world; that thirty-three acres became our backyard and our playground. I used to hunt out there and had the time of my life. It wasn't exactly like back home in Italy and being able to roam the fruit-tree-covered hillsides. After all, my corner of western Pennsylvania is a world away from Piglio. But it was a great experience. I kept some of the land on the side for about half a dozen plum trees, which I still have today.

It was about this time that God spoke to me in a way I will never forget. I had taken a long drive to get a part for a machine I'd bought several years earlier. It was a piece of construction equipment, and the local store I had purchased it from had since gone out of business.

It was March, and there was still some snow on the ground as I drove down the highway to the town, more than an hour away. I had just gotten to a stretch of the road that went over a river before it went between two mountains. It was a beautiful area.

As I was driving through that day, it seemed like everything changed before my eyes. Where usually there were just a few scattered houses, now I saw many beautiful homes decorated as if it were Christmastime. It was a gorgeous scene, like a postcard.

And then a mist or fog seemed to envelop everything and I could hear beautiful music, and as I looked I could see what seemed like an orchestra almost swallowed up by the foggy air. There was a strip of pink-colored cloud among the mist, the type you can see during a sunset, and I could see just the bows of the violinists popping up above the clouds as they were slid back and forth over the strings. The musicians seemed to be on some sort of plateau, but one that was above the earth itself—I could see the shadow it seemed to cast on the road below.

I can't really say what such a sight might mean. In fact, the whole thing lasted maybe ten seconds, but it was stunning and impressive and it touched my heart. If I had been in the passenger seat, I would have assumed I was dreaming, but I was driving at the time so I'm positive I was awake. Many times since, I've taken a drive and gone back down that road, hoping that the vision might appear again. It never has, but the memory of it makes me smile.

It is an experience that reminds me of how much God is present in the world, how He is always by our side. I try always to be open to the signs of His presence; it helps keeps my faith strong.

It was an emotional time, watching my children leave to build homes and lives of their own, and in the mid-1980s, our first grandchild, Alessandra, was born.

There is almost no greater joy than becoming a grandparent for the first time and Alessandra brought a light to our life that was sorely needed, especially in the darkness that had been left by the loss of our precious Lorenzo.

Seeing Maria with that beautiful baby was like seeing the sparkle return to my beloved wife. Lorenzo's death seemed to knock ten years off her life before any of us could even blink. I do not even remember seeing her smile.

But when Alessandra was born all that changed. I began to sing again myself, Maria appeared to come back to life and things seemed to get back on track again. Alessandra would look at us with her big, brown eyes and it made all the world a pleasure to be in.

In those days Gabriella and her husband had to work often, and Alessandra would spend the day with Maria and me. It brought a special happiness to our house to see this little girl grow and explore before our eyes. And the more grandchildren who entered our lives, the more that joy expanded until it filled every corner of our lives.

I had started to realize that even though I had years of hard work and a proven track record of success under my belt, so many people still underestimated me—even my own lawyer. Around that time interest rates at the bank were quite high, and they were running an advertising campaign saying that if anyone opened an account with $100,000, the bank would pay twelve percent interest.

I was curious about that offer and went to my lawyer for advice.

"How sound is that bank? Can I trust them?" I asked.

"Don't you know you have to have a hundred thousand dollars to do that?" he said.

When I told him that I did know, and that I had that kind of money, he was speechless. But after that moment, his demeanor toward me changed and our relationship was never the same. It was a reaction that, even though I didn't really understand it, I had seen once before, with my first boss in Italy. When I had told him how much I enjoyed the work he was teaching me, he'd viewed me as competition and begun to freeze me out. I was stunned to feel like the same thing was happening with this lawyer, especially because I had worked with him for years and he was the one who had helped me gain my financial success. I was so surprised by his reaction, it made me start to wonder if there was something going on behind my back. I never worked with him again.

Even the brothers who agreed to sell me a piece of

the farm—I believe that what they really wanted was to give me a chance to fail. They almost got what they wanted.

It got to the point where real estate was so bad, and things got so tough, that I could not make the payments. Under our agreement, I should have been able to walk away with a certain amount of the land in my name, using the money I had already paid toward those acres. But those brothers refused to abide by our agreement; they wouldn't release the acres I had already paid off. I wasn't about to walk away without a fight, though. What they were doing was unfair and manipulative, so I went to a new lawyer and we went to court.

It was as if those brothers were wolves and thought I was a helpless cow that they could manipulate into a vulnerable position before they pounced. That was not the case.

But things were not immediately resolved. The judge heard the case but it took years before a decision would be made. In the meantime, I kept working. As the years flew by and my claim to part of the farm was left in legal limbo, I continued to buy land and build homes despite the struggling economy.

In 1988 Maria and I found a piece of land nearby, in a township about ten miles away. At first we didn't like it. It seemed like it was too far away from everything, as if it were out in the middle of nowhere. But it was a pretty piece of land, and it was in a wonderful school district, and I started to think a lot about its potential.

I wanted to make an offer to purchase it, about eighteen acres. But Maria wasn't really in favor of it, and we weren't sure if we could get people interested in buying homes there because it was so far away from everything. Finally, I was able to convince Maria that we should go for it, and I made an offer and got the land for $195,000.

I had been hoping to sell lots there for at least $35,000 each, to make the whole project viable—even though at the time lots in that area were selling for closer to $50,000. But as time went on it became clear that no one was coming around looking to build houses out there, and I was starting to worry.

Money was starting to get tight and contractors were starting to approach me, offering to contract out the lots to build houses for spec. The banker warned me to steer clear of that strategy, but I knew I had to do something, so I talked to one of the contractors.

"Why don't you make me an offer for what you think the land is worth?" I said.

He seemed scared, and then he offered me $45,000. I took a few days to think about it because while the offer was $10,000 more than the minimum I had thought of in my mind, it was still low. But, I knew that I could wait no longer and that we had to get started, so I accepted and that man quickly started building the first house on those eighteen acres.

I took the $45,000 and put it in the bank so I could get a mortgage to build a house on the land as well. Even though that offer was low it set things in motion because in short order there were two houses being built on that parcel. Then, things started to happen, and real estate agents started coming around. In the end, I only sold one other lot to another contractor—and was able to sell the lots and build the rest of the homes there myself.

Eventually I created twenty-eight lots to construct houses on, all out of those eighteen acres. The project was so profitable that by the time I was done it helped me get back on my feet financially and put me in a prime position to negotiate with the brothers who owned that farm I had been fighting for.

The legal case was dragging on and I got quite impatient. I had been working with my lawyer but was consistently frustrated with how long it was taking to work things out. I was always trying to move things along and sometimes reached out to the brothers to make them an offer or try to negotiate. At one point, the brothers tried to make me an offer and give me only a tiny portion of the farm—the worst piece of it, actually.

I didn't take the deal. At one point I was so angry

with the slow pace of things I went to my new lawyer, demanding to know why he wasn't doing anything more to move things along and why the judge was taking so long.

It was quite a lesson in patience. The lawyer said that there was nothing to be done and no real way to control or influence the judge. The decision would be made when the judge was ready to make it, he said, and not any sooner. But he encouraged me to take it easy.

"If you can wait, and you have the money in your pocket and can just leave things alone, they'll end up coming to you and you'll have an advantage," he explained. "Then you can settle things the way you want them."

I could see his point, so that was what I tried to do, but it wasn't easy. It took a decade before the judge made a decision—ten long years I waited—but the result was in my favor and the judge enforced the original agreement, giving me possession of the acres I had already paid for.

It was 1988 or 1989 then, and little did those brothers know it but their effort to get the better of me, to see me fail, had totally backfired. That case had given me time to regroup, to regain my financial strength, and it turned out that my lawyer was right—now I was the one with the upper hand.

When the judge enforced the original agreement

and released my portion of the farm to me, it made me a partner with those brothers. Now they had to negotiate with me, and they suddenly wanted to discuss what we would do with the rest of the land. And they weren't even looking around at the bigger picture. That farm was in such a strategic location, close to a growing community with jobs and good roads, that the value of the place had actually increased while those brothers had waged their petty battle against me.

There was a big industrial park near the farm, and I had already learned that a contract had been signed and a road was going to be built nearby. I made my move and told the brothers that I wanted to buy the rest of the farm, and at the same rate as our previous deal.

"I will give you fifty thousand dollars now," I told them, "and I'll pay another hundred seventy-five thousand over five years, with interest."

After some negotiation, we agreed to change things just a little bit. I put down $75,000 with another $150,000 plus interest to pay over the next five years. That was $30,000 a year in payments, but I knew what I was doing.

They eventually agreed, but from the start they got a judgment. It was clear that they still had negative intentions toward me. That judgment was a like getting permission from the court before something ever happened and it said that if I missed even one payment, they could swoop in and take all the land back to satisfy the mortgage and could even go farther, taking my other assets to satisfy the judgment. I did not let them intimidate me or try to bully me. I knew where I stood.

I'll never forget that day in 1990, in the lawyer's office, when they explained over and over again the terms of the deal as if I didn't or couldn't understand the magnitude of what they were saying.

The lawyer representing those brothers was a bit taken aback by my certainty and kept asking if I understood. He even talked to my lawyer as if I weren't there, urging my lawyer to make sure I understood—but I never wavered. I knew I had good income; I knew I had other resources too. I just kept saying "yes."

But they were so cocky and so sure of themselves—and so sure that I wouldn't be able to hold up my end of the bargain—that they didn't take my certainty as a warning sign. They agreed to the arrangement and in the end, I wound up the owner of all 125 acres.

It was a key acquisition both in the community and in my plans and dreams. Owning that much land meant that I was more than a contractor or small-time developer. It meant that I could start to think of projects on a bigger scale, to move forward, to really have a major impact on the community.

A few years later, Maria and I attended a Fourth of July party. By then, two of the brothers I had been dealing with had died.

One of the other brothers was at the party. And by coincidence, we ended up in the same room.

He had been drinking and was really rather friendly, despite everything that had happened between us. After a little while the other people in the room filed out and we found ourselves alone.

That man was a bit tipsy and he started telling me things he probably never thought he would share—confirming my suspicions of what had been going on all along.

"We couldn't believe you could make those payments," the brother said, laughing. "We wanted to destroy you. We wanted to see you ruined."

I am sure that later on, when he sobered up, he was shocked to realize what he had told me, what he had admitted to. As it turned out, he and I became good friends, but his admission made me realize that no matter how much I tried to serve God, no matter how successful I was, there were still elements that tried to get in my way.

But that is the benefit of dedicating your will and intention to God. It doesn't make you immune from the small minds and evil hearts of others, but it always seems like whenever anyone tries to hurt me or do me harm, they end up only hurting themselves. The trials people tried to put me through only helped make me stronger and only helped me get what I wanted in the end.

It is not admirable to enjoy the pain and suffering of others, but I have to admit that watching the people who tried to do me wrong end up suffering themselves has given me a certain degree of gratitude. I never purposely set out to harm anyone, but watching those brothers get what they deserved and end up having to give up that farm to me was quite satisfying. If people want to do the wrong thing, if people want to follow a path of evil and harm others, then let them go to hell. I am happy to sit by and watch it happen.

Meanwhile, as all of this was going on, I was watching my son grow up and branch out on his own. David had been working with me at the property while he'd finished his degree at Case Western Reserve University. He'd been doing manual labor for me, digging ditches and shoveling.

David had always been a bit of a stubborn kid. When he'd started college, he'd been determined to keep hunting even though it was interfering with his classes. He would come home for the weekend just to make sure he could go out and hunt, insisting that nothing was going to make him stop. But by the end of his first year, he hadn't been doing so well. So, he'd made a decision to hunker down and put school first, and he'd ended up graduating on time and doing very well.

But at this point he was still trying to figure out what he wanted to do with his future. I watched him work for a few days and while he was a great worker, what I saw didn't make me happy at all. He was so smart and capable, he could have been a stock broker or anything he wanted, though I must admit I liked the idea of his following in my footsteps and becoming a builder like me.

But what I was seeing then was an intelligent, young kid working in the dirt. It unnerved me. Maria encouraged me to leave him alone and let him make up his own mind. One day he came to me and said he had decided to stay there, in Pennsylvania. He asked me what his job would be.

"You know what your job is," I told him. "You do everything. You do everything that I do."

David's working with me, just going along project to project, was not ideal for the long run, though. He needed to do something about his future. The more I thought about it the more I realized that I needed to do something.

What am I going to do? I thought. *What is he going to do working for me like that?*

So one day I decided to surprise him. I told him that I didn't like him doing labor like that.

"What? You mean after all of that I'm out of a job?" he said, looking confused. I laughed and shook my head.

"I'm going to take you to the bank and I'm going to co-sign with you so you can get a mortgage in your name."

I told him that I would give him a lot on which he could build a house, and that he would be responsible not only for the construction but for selling it too. He could pay me back for the lot and everything else once he made his sale. To help him get started, I also paid him a small weekly salary.

He loved the idea. He was his own boss, and it was a great opportunity to help my son begin his career in such a solid way.

In fact, he was so eager he got himself in trouble with the law! He sprinted off to find out what he needed to do to get a permit but ended up coming home a little too quickly. I knew that something was wrong, and when I asked what had happened he admitted he had gotten stopped by the police because he had been speeding. The cops let him off with a warning, but I decided to have some fun with him.

"Maybe you're not quite as ready as I thought," I said, trying to hold in my laughter. "Maybe you should wait another six months?"

"No, I'm ready," he insisted.

He did so well on that first project he had $40,000 to spare and wanted to begin another one quickly. That time, though, I knew we had to take the training wheels off. I told him I wouldn't be co-signing the loan for this mortgage, that he didn't need me like that anymore.

However, other people didn't quite see it that way. The day he went to the bank to sign the paperwork, the manager looked around.

"Where's your father?" the bank manager asked.

"My father's not here," David said. "He's not going to sign."

"Then there's no mortgage," the banker said.

David was pretty upset and called me immediately. I told him to hold the phone close enough to that banker so that the banker could hear what I was about to say.

"If I need to give another signature, I'm going to take my business and go to another bank!" I said.

The banker gulped, and before I was even off the phone he had put the paperwork for David's loan through. David was on his way.

Gabriella, by this time, had two kids of her own and was working as a CPA. Paula was also married by this time and was a mother who was working as a doctor of optometry.

It is a special thing to plant something and take care of it, nurture it, protect it as it grows. There is nothing like being a parent. It is the ultimate gift that we give both to ourselves and the world.

Mother Nature and all her glorious scenery can seem so accidental, so haphazard. After all, what factors contribute to a picturesque countryside, an infinite blue sky, a tall, strong tree? What makes a flower beautiful or a piece of fruit delectable? Is it all an accident of fate?

I do not believe that the beauty and power of our world is simply or only an act of chance. Mother Nature's glory is powered by the endless love and wisdom of God, an authority too great to be accidental.

And so it is with people and how we live our lives. There are some people who go through life as if there is no bigger picture, as if what they do and how they act doesn't matter. These people often squander the good around them whether they are born with strong foundations and roots and loving families or not. They stumble around with the worst attitude of all: that the quality of their lives and experiences is beyond their control. Nothing could be further from the truth.

Our potential depends both on how we begin our lives and how we conduct ourselves in the duration. Like a strong tree that bears fruit for generations, some of our destiny is determined by chance—being rooted in rich soil, having access to the proper amount of sunlight, not being undermined by disease or insects. But having a good, productive life is not determined only by chance. Human beings have so much more opportunity before them; so much of our lives is shaped by our choices, by our decisions to use the nutrients and goodness around us for good, and by how we respond to the difficulties we face.

In the late 1990s I saw how the goodness that we

put out can come back and reward us. The local Italian-American society had often invited me over the years to become a member, though I'd never fully accepted their invitation. Partly, I knew that if I went to their meetings often, I would just end up eating too much! And, partly, it was because I'd always preferred to spend my extra time with my family, with Maria and the kids, more than anywhere else. I was never one to spend a lot of time away, just hanging out with the guys.

Each year the Italian-American society honored a few local Italian residents and they had tried for several years to recognize me in that way, but it was not until 1998 that I was given the award.

I went down there for the ceremony in May of 1998, and it was a wonderful night. They gave me a plaque with my picture on it and honored me for founding what I by now had called the Countryside Heights Company. It was a special day, a day of pride for me, on which I felt like the community I had called home for so many years was giving me a pat on the back for all the hard work I had done over the years.

It was a beautiful plaque, and in part it reads:

> After immigrating to the United States, through his ingenuity, skill and hard work he has established himself as a quality developer and builder in founding the Countryside Heights

> Company and bringing honor to the Italian-American community.
>
> Presented this 17th day of May, nineteen hundred and ninety eight.

I had come a long way from the days in which the bank had refused to loan me money because I did not fit their definition of a builder, or those times in which my lack of skill with the English language had made it tough for me to get bids. It was a nice validation to receive from my community after all those years of effort, projects and work.

The best people can take the good that surrounds them and use it to grow, to change for the better, to dream and to achieve that dream as much as they can. It is hard work, as we must be ever-vigilant against the things that would derail us such as anger and grief, laziness and fear. With faith, with love and hard work, we can make it through.

Certainly there are many who never reach their goals. Sadly, there are too many people beaten down by life and circumstance who never even have the opportunity to dream big in the first place. And then there are some who don't seem to change no matter how many years have gone by.

It was around this time that Maria and I took a trip back home to Italy, and it is one I will never forget, though not for happy reasons. In years past, we had gone home somewhat regularly, but after Lorenzo had died, we'd let a lot of time go by before we felt we could or wanted to.

So this was our first journey home in many years, and I had the shock of my life one day while I was talking to my sister.

It seemed as though I wasn't the only one in my family with a penchant for buying up properties. I had known, of course, that my parents had purchased land when we'd moved from Piglio to Anzio. It was a piece of land we called La Valle.

When I'd left Italy to come to America, I'd been twenty-six years old, but my sister had been just eighteen. I knew very well how much of a bully our brother, Orlando, was, but I had never known how far he had gone in his efforts to intimidate our family—the very people he should have been loving and protecting.

Sitting together on that warm day, basking in the Italian sun, my sister told me that Orlando had done everything possible to take as much of La Valle for himself even though it was not meant to be solely his. Orlando had tried to take or use my part of the land because I wasn't there, and he had taken my sister's piece of the property from her, but he had done more than that. He had beaten her up—more than once.

To hear my sister tell me this so many years later, after so much life had gone by, did nothing to lessen the anger I felt. Orlando had always done whatever he'd wanted, but to know that he had used his fists on our sister for the sake of being intimidating… That was nothing that anyone should have tolerated. He should have been in jail for that but now, after all this time had passed, Orlando was looking to capitalize on his ill-begotten gains once again. He was in the process of trying to put that property into his son's name. Orlando had told so many lies and was so intimidating to those around him that no one wanted to fight him. They were too scared.

I wasn't afraid of him. And hearing what he had done to our sister made me want to give him what he deserved. I had a big argument with him, but he never had the courage to say anything back. I knew I couldn't let him get away with doing whatever he wanted with that property, and I would never stoop to his level of intimidation. But I did something better. I went to a lawyer, who at first told me there was nothing that could be done because too much time had gone by.

But then we discovered a law in Italy that says that if the property was taken by violent means, we would have some recourse. The fact that he had beaten our sister so many times just to get his hands on that land meant that we could fight him in court.

No one else had the money to fight him and because they were scared, they were almost willing to let it go. But I had the money and the property, which is just a couple of miles from the beach, is now worth some money. But for me, it's not about the money. I made a promise to all of my brothers and sisters that I would take care of the lawyer and that we were going to finally take a stand against Orlando's horrible actions. It wasn't right that he should be rewarded for something he'd gained by hurting everyone around him.

He thought everything was going to go smoothly for himself. It probably would have if not for me. But I could never forgive him for beating up my sister, for taking what wasn't his in such an awful way.

It seems that Orlando, from the very start, had something wrong with him. He had never seemed to absorb the love and lessons of our parents but had been resentful and twisted in his thinking even as a youth. It goes to show that even the best parents cannot always produce children who see the world as they do.

Having children, in a way, is the greatest risk a person can take because we do not have control over who they become or what happens to them. But it is most certainly also the greatest miracle. People, if they are very lucky and are able to have children, can take what they know and pass it on to them. There is something so special about helping a human being not only to explore and learn about the world around them, but to help them grow into the best person they can be.

If a person puts the same faith and effort into one's family as they do their work, a beautiful thing begins to happen. Maria and I always worked as hard as we could, spent as much time as we could with our kids, because that was where we wanted to be, and that was what we wanted to do. Losing our oldest son, Lorenzo, had left a permanent scar, like a lightning bolt that strikes a tree, destroying it.

But we never let the grief cripple our family, and the loss of Lorenzo only made the five of us closer. Our three remaining children grew up into strong and loving adults with whom we are still close. Seeing them achieve their own success, having their own children and making their own families—there has been nothing more satisfying. Singing Italian songs to my little grandchildren, telling them stories and joking around with them, I now know what my father-in-law must have felt when he cared for young Gabriella in those months when I was still in Italy.

As my children were finding their own ways in the world and planting their own roots, I was poised to make my biggest professional dream a reality. Five short years after making that second agreement with the brothers who owned the 125-acre farm, I had paid off my debt. I now owned all of that land despite the nasty intentions of those who really, in their hearts, wanted nothing more than for me to fail.

When I looked at that 125 acres I saw nothing but potential. I started planning for the largest development I had ever sought to make. I called it Countryside Heights.

At that time, since we had just finished paying off the property, we were somewhat cash-poor, though the value of the property meant that we were doing just fine. It also helped that I had such a good relationship with the bank, where I had massive borrowing power. I had spent a lot of time talking with Maria and David about what houses we should build on the farm and what type of development it would be—whether we would go with townhouses, less-expensive homes in the $150,000 range, or something else.

Some people encouraged me to go with a less-expensive type of home, saying that they would sell so fast it would be worth it. I wasn't sure I wanted to go that route, though.

But the more I thought about it, the more I knew that I wanted to do something different. I leaned toward building homes at Countryside Heights that were similar to what I had made at the earlier development: bigger, nicer, more expensive homes.

But there was another snag—an industrial park with medical and professional offices that was being built right next door. In the bigger picture I looked at that industrial park as a huge asset, a place for people to work close to my development.

In terms of building houses, though, the industrial park represented a bit of a dilemma. Because of that I wasn't sure where to build the first house at Countryside Heights, but I took a risk and started construction on a $245,000 home on a lot adjacent to the industrial park. I felt that if I built that house in the center of the development, that it would make any homes I later built on the outer edges of the property less attractive. I left a fifty-foot buffer between my land and the industrial park and started to build.

Without even knowing it the developers at the industrial park were helping me out—part of what they were constructing there was townhouses, homes that were nice but all attached, and they were offering them for around $220,000. But for just a little bit more money at nearby Countryside Heights, people could get big, gorgeous houses on their own lots. My business there did and is still doing quite well, especially since there is no other place quite like it in the whole area. It was special, and its unique nature ensured that we did quite well.

Eventually, Countryside Heights had 240 lots with large, gorgeous homes selling for hundreds of thousands of dollars. In fact, we have not even come close to finishing the development. These days, I sell the lots while David builds the homes.

Things were going very well for my family in America, but back in Italy this wasn't the case. My younger brother was sick, and had been for a long time. I spent a lot of time on the phone with him, talking to him and trying to help him.

He hadn't had the easiest life. He'd tried to do what

he thought God wanted, tried to live in the pleasure of God, but as I would listen to him tell his stories or talk about his decisions I knew that he didn't really understand what it meant to live in the service of the Lord. He was in construction as well and had at one time made a lot of money. He had bought a big piece of equipment that could move large amounts of earth, and he would use it to dig out basements for people.

But then he'd made a business decision that had ended up doing him in. He'd bought another one of those machines—they were quite expensive—and made an agreement with his brother-in-law, thinking that God wanted him to make more money and that this was the way he would be serving the Lord. In fact, he thought that God would approve of his taking on that partner, but he didn't seem to understand the difference between generosity and giving away too much. Things didn't work out. I told him to be careful, and warned him that he shouldn't step on God's feet, or play God himself.

"If God wants you to do something, he'll do it," I told him. "The pleasure of God is not like that."

He ended up in large amounts of debt and by the time he got so sick, nothing had worked out for him the way it should have. When he did pass away, it was a sad time in my life.

But there was only so much that I could do for him. He was an adult, living his own life, and he was half a world away when all this was going on. It was one of the most difficult times in my life, to find myself on the phone while my younger brother suffered so much.

Life is full of ups and downs. And while the family I grew up with was enduring its own trials, things at home in America were not nearly as difficult.

There was so much good in my life. Countryside Heights had begun, and we were building beautiful homes there. Our children were college-educated, grown up, married and having children of their own.

It was a peaceful life. Whenever I looked around the garden of my life, at the fruits of my labor—our home, our kids, my business, my success—I felt as if everything represented the picture of health. It was as if there were nothing but lush greenery and beautiful sunshine, gentle breezes and blue skies.

I felt as though it was time for me to do something for myself, something I had longed to do since I'd been a child in Italy. I decided to go back to school. I had spent so much time as a kid worrying about my lack of education, and even though it didn't end up holding me back in my work I felt like I wanted to do what I could to improve my English skills and get a diploma.

The schoolwork itself wasn't too hard, but I did find it difficult to sit in a classroom in the spring and summer, when it was so bright and beautiful outside. So my first attempt at taking classes was cut short when I found myself distracted by nature's beauty.

The second time around I went back to take classes at a local technical school, to earn my general equivalency diploma. I was sixty-five years old and took some time away from work so that I could attend classes. I started in January, with a teacher who was only in his late twenties. But I was able to breeze through most of the material and by April or May of 2001 I had passed all my tests and gotten my GED.

Finally, years after I'd been forced to quit school with just a fifth-grade education, I had achieved a personal dream. It was a proud moment.

It was around this time that I was also eyeing another piece of land. The farm I'd bought and used to make Countryside Heights was a large property, one I often went hunting on with my friends and family, but as I built up my development I found it more and more difficult to go hunting there.

I had to tell my friends and family it was no longer a good place for the sport, it wasn't good for the people living there. But there was a large farm in a neighboring county, just about thirty miles from my house, that had caught my eye. It was rugged land with few decent roads. I wasn't exactly looking to create another development and don't think it would have been exactly right for that purpose anyway.

When the land went up for sale the owners, who had been in bankruptcy, originally asked for $500,000, which was well beyond what I wanted to spend. After a while the land did not sell and they dropped the price. I began to negotiate with them but at first they gave me a bit of a hard time. I guess they thought I really wasn't interested after all. Finally, I got them to drop the price to $195,000. It was still a little more than I wanted to spend but not nearly as much as the original asking price; in the end I got 318 acres for $613 apiece, and now my family and friends have a place where we love to hunt and spend time.

As the years went on I was stronger in my beliefs. My faith in God was solid, my work ethic unwavering. I cared about what was right, what was true; I never put petty issues before God's will. It was not the easiest road, to put quality before profit, people's feelings before what was best for me or my business. It was difficult to work so much, to be away from my family so often, because I was working two jobs. But I did everything that I did because of my love for them and for God. It kept me going even when times were tough.

Without Maria, I could not have achieved what I did. I loved her with a feeling so deep, it seemed like it leapt straight out of my heart. I couldn't help but love her. She was my rock, the mother of my children, the one who kept everything grounded and our home happy, and she made it possible for me to work like that. I couldn't have achieved what I did without her. I never wanted anyone else and felt that I had proven my fidelity both in words, actions and feelings.

But little did I know that there were bad things hiding among the otherwise vibrant vegetation of the garden of my life. It's not that I felt like life was perfect. I still had troubles with my brother-in-law; it still grated on my nerves that so many people seemed to have it out for me. Over time some weeds had wound their way into the roots of my life and grown up right alongside everything else, but had stayed hidden just out of my sight. They might not have been obvious to me, but they were doing damage all along.

As the years went by my brother-in-law's attitude and behavior had become worse and more insulting. It had started out with that strange episode long before, when he had insinuated that I was sleeping with his wife even though nothing could be further from the truth. He thought he had me under his thumb because I never lashed out at him when he was being boorish, but really, I was just doing my best to ignore his actions.

He thought nothing of hunting on my lands whenever he pleased or cursing at me in my own home. He was so jealous of me and everything I had, it would have been funny if it wasn't so rude. He would often bother my son, calling him and asking him for things that he wanted instead of coming to me directly, and his behavior put David in an awkward spot.

He wouldn't even ask me for help. When he had health problems, including a bad heart, and had killed a deer while hunting on my property, he loaded the animal on his truck himself rather than deign to ask me to assist him.

Pasqualino had always tried to push me around. He had a concealed weapon permit and would always find a way to talk to me in an intimidating manner when we were alone. He tried to make it a joke, telling me not to "mess with the guy with the gun."

One year, when my wife was throwing a big birthday party for their mother at our house, he tried to bully me. The party had gone well and afterwards some of us were sitting around the table, including my mother-in-law, Pasqualino and his wife, Assunta, Gloria and Maria and I, when all of a sudden he jumped up and got in my face, shouting and cursing the name of God in Italian.

I was pretty angry but it takes me a long time to lash out at someone who is trying to hurt me. This time, Maria intervened before I could do or say anything.

"Pasqualino, you cannot say those words in my house," she told him.

He was such a bully that no one else said anything or tried to talk to him about his behavior. Some time later, he came over to borrow a bucket of topsoil and Maria invited him in for a drink.

Don't you know, we were all three of us sitting around at the table, and he did it again? Out of nowhere he stood up, bent over and got in my face.

"*Porco dio!*" he shouted.

I'd had enough.

I raised my fist and slammed it down on the table so hard I nearly broke it.

"*BASTA!*" I shouted. "Don't you ever talk like this at my table again. This is the table where I teach my kids about God, and where we eat and pray. Don't take the name of the Lord in vain here."

"I'm sorry, I'm sorry," Pasqualino said, shaking and shrinking back in a pathetic way. "I didn't think you were like that."

"Like what?" I said. But it was clear what he meant. He never thought I would stand up for myself, or that I was strong enough as a person to fight him. Because I'd never lashed out at him, he thought it was OK to bully me—just like that neighborhood kid.

But even my standing up to him wasn't enough to get him to change his ways. He felt that he was so superior, nothing much made a dent in his behavior.

Pasqualino and my friends and relatives often used my land for hunting trips on the weekend, a practice that did not usually bother me. I was happy to let them do so, to let them share what I had.

One weekend I took a drive down to the property, where there was a house I had restored. Almost everyone would stay there for overnight trips, though Pasqualino would often arrive early in the morning on the day of the hunt. When I pulled up I saw my son-in-law, Patrick, packing up his truck. I asked him what was going on.

"Well, I'm going to hunt on my own property," he said.

"Why?" I said.

"Little Pietro wants to go home," he said, referring to my thirteen-year-old grandson.

As I questioned him, he explained that the previous night, the group that was to go hunting that weekend, including Pasqualino and his adult son, had gotten together to discuss which position everyone would take. And while they were doing that, Pasqualino had decided that the best spot—one that my grandson was going to use—should go to his own son, a grown man, instead.

I was boiling mad.

"Why didn't you tell him to go to hell?" I asked my son-in-law.

Patrick tried to calm me down and said that he just didn't want to fight with anyone or have any problems. He asked me not to make a big deal of it and said he'd take care of it some other way, later on.

I told him that I would, but this was too much of an insult for me to let go. I marched into the cabin and asked the guys inside for a magic marker or grease pencil, something for me to write with.

Then I stood there and wrote on a board that I hung on the wall. I talked as I wrote, right in front of Pasqualino's face.

> Don't push my children and grandchildren around.
>
> Me, The Boss
> David

And I hung it on the wall.

Pasqualino jumped up nervously, asking if he had done anything wrong.

"If you didn't do anything wrong you have nothing to worry about," I told him, quietly seething. "But if you did do something wrong, then go to hell!"

The next weekend, I went down to the cabin myself, but Pasqualino didn't dare show his face and I was glad for it. I wanted nothing to do with him. I was done.

A cousin of ours, from my wife's side of the family, came by that day and tried to ask in an innocent way where Pasqualino was.

"Pasqualino doesn't like the way things are run," I said. "He's not going to come anymore."

It seemed like the cousin was feeling things out so that he could report back to Pasqualino, but I wasn't going to budge one bit.

As time went on I stood firm. I refused to attend family gatherings at Pasqualino's house, and anytime we saw him out in the community I just ignored him. Like any bully, he didn't like that one bit and would try to talk to me each time. I'd be at a party and go to get a drink or something to eat and he'd run over to my side, smiling at me in a friendly way and following me around. But I just turned my back.

Not surprisingly, this caused a bit of a problem with Maria. She got quite angry with me.

"I do all this stuff for your family and you can't even say 'hi' to my brother?" she said.

Finally, I just told her the truth.

"Maria, I don't know what I'm going to do," I said. "You've got to choose. I can't live like this anymore. I don't want to lose you, but I don't want to live like a jackass either."

"I don't want to lose you either," she said quietly.

And after that, she didn't push for me to be friendly with Pasqualino again.

But my brother-in-law's attitude was not the only problem undermining my family. I was stunned to learn that for decades, my family's health and happiness had been undermined by evil rumors, by a situation that I'd thought had been resolved so long ago, I had nearly forgotten about it.

I was talking to my daughter, Paula, one day on the phone. She had been planning a family event for one of her children, I can't quite remember what—either a First Communion or a birthday party, one of those important days when usually a whole family comes together to celebrate. But Paula was irritated and voiced her frustration in a surprising way.

"I'd like to invite Zia Gloria, but I can't because of you," she said.

I was angry and confused all at once. What she was saying disturbed me so much, I wasn't sure what to make of it at first but in a heartbeat I knew that Gloria's evil was somehow, some way, nearly thirty years later, still lingering.

Emotion took over and I slammed that telephone into the wall with fury.

"What did you say? What do you mean?" I burst out angrily.

Paula immediately backed off.

"I'm sorry, I'm sorry, never mind," she said.

But it was too late. I finally knew that something had been going on.

I felt duped. I felt as if I had been living with a curtain pulled over my eyes all those years, and as if Gloria were still working her deceptions and jealousies backstage with the ultimate goal of ruining me somehow. To realize that my family, my children, thought less of me because of this situation—or worse, that I was not worthy of their love and faith—was a body blow I could not take.

I began to look around at my life with a more critical eye. Suddenly I started to see the weeds among the flowers, so to speak. My son, David, had always seemed to have an attitude with me, one I couldn't explain. Maybe this was why? Did he think I had betrayed his mother and our family? If this thinking, these rumors about me, had been going on since that upsetting night with Gloria, that meant it was something he had lived with his entire life.

Maria knew the truth; she had seen what was going on with her own eyes. But could it be that after all this time Gloria was somehow still creating trouble? After all, I often worked long hours, and it can be tough to stand strong in the face of devilry that is so constant.

Throughout my life, I have endured the pain that others would inflict on me, but it always took a lot for me to lash out, to return the pain. Even as a child, how many times had I walked past that neighborhood bully? I can't even tell you. I simply had tried to ignore his rudeness, his abuse, and go about my business in a way that was best for me. This is, after all, what we are taught to do: to turn the other cheek, to treat people the way that we would like to be treated ourselves, regardless of the actions of others.

And that is how I always tried to be, the rule I tried to live by. People could step on my feet and I would pretend not to be hurting. Years earlier, Maria and I had been at a party being thrown by our daughter-in-law's family. We had been friendly with them; my daughter-in-law's sister would always say "hello." Yet there was a moment at that party I haven't been able to forget.

It had been a barbecue and I had been sitting at a

table, eating, when this girl had come up with some of her friends. She'd had a bottle of wine in her hands and was passing it around, filling everyone's cups. But she'd completely ignored me. She'd stood up and made a toast and everybody had drunk their wine, but I'd sat there like a donkey. I hadn't said or done anything, but it definitely had hurt me to be ignored like that.

As I thought about the situation, I became sure that the girl's behavior had been a sign that the nasty rumors that were undermining my family had perhaps been heard by others as well. And I think that this girl was, in her own way, judging me based on that. But I don't blame her; at least she had the guts to react that way to someone she thought was doing wrong.

Little situations like that happen to people every day. Maybe someone else would have said something or acted angrily because of it, but I didn't. I've often found that in moments when I've felt hurt or abused by people, it's been just another sign, another way for evil to tempt me into doing the wrong thing. I found along the way, though, that I was facing more than garden-variety indignities. I didn't just have people who were stepping on my feet, but stepping on my feet again and again, causing damage and pain—and still I did my best to endure.

But I am only a human being. And sometimes I reach my breaking point.

With the neighborhood bully, when I could no

longer deal with his intimidations, I'd lost my temper and knocked his block off. But this time, this nasty, degrading set of lies had wormed its way into the heart of my home. It had been there for years.

It was as if I had spent my life in a tug of war between good and evil, with evil always working hard to bait me and try to sway me from my faith and my intentions. Usually I didn't find it too difficult to stay on the side of good, and to see evil for what it was.

As I thought about it, I came to one of the saddest conclusions of my life. I began to think that I could not hold my wife or kids responsible for this situation. It was not their fault.

After all, if your sister is going to talk to you like this, for as long as this had been going on, how could you not believe her even just a little bit? How could anyone not believe their own sister? How could I blame Maria for doubting me when these rumors came from her own family?

The more I thought, the more I realized that there was nothing for me to do. I couldn't remove this evil, not by myself. If I walked out or in some other way tried to ruin my family or lash out, it wouldn't do any good to anyone, least of all myself.

I became depressed and as time went on it only got worse. I started distancing myself from everyone and living in a sort of cocoon.

I lost interest in my life and felt so lost. If I did not

have the respect and faith of my family anymore, what did I have? It was a dark time, and it was starting to show outwardly.

We spent most winters in Florida, and about this time I started going out by myself to go fishing. Once, there was a group of Italians nearby, fishing and talking. I listened to them for a while and then tried to start a conversation with them, but they seemed a little surprised.

"I thought you were homeless," one of the men said.

It was clear then how far I had fallen, but it wasn't enough to shake me out of my bad feeling. I had worked so hard for so long, and now it felt like it had all been for nothing.

Some people might have thought that idea was ridiculous. After all, by this time I was doing quite well with the business, we had a nice home and I had plenty of money. But I never worked like I did just to get money. That was never my goal or my motivation. I had always worked toward a dream, but the key part of that dream was the success and well-being of my wife and kids. Without them, nothing seemed worth it.

I just couldn't understand why this was happening, and why it was happening to me. I leaned heavily on my faith in God but for a while even that didn't seem to help as I felt adrift in a sea of dark feeling.

I started to think about things that I hadn't thought

about in years—things that seem small in hindsight but, while I was in the depths of my depression, were hurtful. Like the woman at the party who hadn't poured me a glass of wine. I mulled it over repeatedly, trying to figure out what had happened, why she had done that. By this time, the young woman had died of cancer, which was quite sad.

But I'll never forget what happened after that. I looked up one day and saw, from far away, a tiny, bright dot. The bright light was moving fast, zooming toward me in an amazing way—just as when I'd seen my father's image on that dreadful night of temptation.

The light slowed down as it approached me, and I could see that it was the woman. She looked beautiful, wearing a cashmere sweater and with her hair and makeup all done. She looked healthy, not anything like she must have been suffering in her last days with the cancer.

The image flashed me a smile so bright and wonderful, it was better than any smile I had seen in all the years I had known her.

"I'm sorry," she said. "I'm so sorry."

I looked at the image of this woman I knew, and looked her in the eye. I didn't say anything, but gave her a smile and a wink of my own. Then, I saw that fantastic smile again and suddenly, she was gone.

It was nothing and everything, like the night I had seen my father's face scolding me with the haunting phrase, "Is this the best you can do?" Certainly, seeing this woman appear before me was a moving experience, though nothing as intense and personal as seeing my father had been. This was, in a way, a reconciliation that soothed the pain of that little hurt. It gave me a sense of peace and calmed some of the darkness that was in my heart at that time. I felt like once again, the good people I had known during my life were somehow watching over me once they'd died, like good angels helping to guide me. Her visit made me feel better. And that was a difficult thing to do, for the bad feeling was hard to overcome.

I would often pray to God, to Jesus, to help me understand and give me hope. One morning I was in the kitchen, which had a little island in it where we could sit, eat and talk. I was by myself; Maria's place was empty. And as I sat, I was thinking and praying to Jesus about my situation as if I were talking right to him. Before I even knew it, I looked up and there was a nice-looking young man sitting in Maria's chair.

It was Jesus, sitting there before me.

Perhaps another man would have been scared, surprised or even a little intimidated. I, however, was a man of faith. And my faith had been my constant companion. In my mind and heart, God was always by my side, helping me through the bad times and motivating me through all the hard work. So, to see the son of God sitting in my kitchen in what felt like one of the worst times of my life was not scary at all.

He was not a big man. He had nice, black hair and a well-kept beard, and I just knew, without even questioning it, that this beautiful young man was God's son. He just smiled.

"What have you got to complain about?" he said, again shining a big, bright smile. "Look what they did to me."

I grew solemn. I just turned my face away. I couldn't look at him anymore. I didn't know what he would say or do, but I didn't hear anything and when I turned back to look at him again he wasn't there.

Maria was starting to get worried. I felt as though there was nothing anybody could do. At that point I felt like it didn't matter if I lived or died because I felt like no one believed me or believed in me—especially Maria, who had seen the situation with her own eyes and still seemed to doubt me. Everything I'd worked for was gone.

Well, when Maria saw that I had gotten that depressed, she realized something had to be done. She did a very brave thing and went to confront her sister.

Gloria denied everything and claimed she had never said anything about me or told any lies that I was after her.

My wife came home and seemed happy though, I think, with just a tiny bit of doubt still in her heart. But then she spoke to Gabriella.

"No, she told me too," Gabriella said. "She told me directly."

Gabriella went to talk to Gloria herself, and at first Gloria held steadfast, continuing to deny that she had ever spread any rumors or done anything wrong. But then as they talked Gabriella just said, "What do you mean? You did tell me."

"I didn't mean it that way," Gloria said at first, suggesting that Gabriella had simply misunderstood, but that did not last for long. And it seemed like for a few minutes, the evil that had been driving this whole situation was gone. Just for a few moments, it was as if the Devil had run away and God seemed to be in Gloria's mouth, and she told the truth.

It was as if the curtain had finally been lifted, and the dark storm clouds that had been oppressing me flew away. The feeling of my family changed and it wasn't long before I became my own self again. I came back to my life, to my family, and things began to right themselves.

After this episode Gloria was finally out of our lives. No one in my family would give her the time of day, and while I feel bad for Maria and her having to deal with that when it came to her sister, I am not too upset about it.

It was about this time that I sold my piece of that property, both the thirty-three acres and the lot on which I had built our second home. We had always wanted to move to Countryside Heights, and finally we did.

I wanted to do something for Maria and so I asked her what kind of house she wanted. She had always worked so hard all her life—for herself, for us, for the kids. All of the homes we'd made for ourselves were beautiful, but I put my heart into this one. She had seen this one house in a magazine. It was a two-story home with six bedrooms, a big deck and an endless view out the back. It had a big garden with a six-foot fence. This home is a little too big for us now, but it is often filled with our children and grandchildren, with laughter and love.

Still, I found there was always evil and the Devil at work somewhere in the world. Even though I had always tried to live my life in a way that was respectful, that valued morals and the good in the world, some people always seemed to have it in for me. They didn't seem to understand.

Just last year, a man I had never seen before showed up where we were building at Countryside Heights. He spoke to me rudely, brusquely, nastily, asking me about "all that money" I had made and how I felt now. I had to talk to him for ten or fifteen minutes before he changed his tune a bit and realized that I was like everybody else. As it turned out, he used to hunt on the land that I'd bought to make Countryside Heights, and he was angry because it had been taken away from him.

Always, I could see around me the tug of war between God and the Devil, between the good and the bad in the world. I have seen so many people fall prey to the darkness of the world either because they didn't try to fight it or because they didn't know, or because their circumstances didn't allow them another option. And I have seen such glorious times, such love and happiness and hope.

And always, it is the light of God's love that nourishes and sustains us as people, that can guide us through the treacherous times and situations life sometimes serves up. Those who are willing to follow their faith and live in the glory of God's love and intention, those who live in the pleasure of God, are not spared from the trials of life. Sometimes, I think that making the decision to put one's life in the hands of the Lord, to live in a way that honors Him and serves Him, makes a person more of a target for the Devil's work.

After all, what a coup it would be for the Devil to successfully tempt someone off their path, especially someone who has chosen to offer his life to God. To see that constant fight between good and evil in the world is one thing; to be caught in its crosshairs can be devastating.

I was lucky to have been given a good, strong

foundation on which to learn the lessons of my life. I was lucky, also, to have the opportunity to make mistakes that taught me those lessons, that helped shape my character without hurting anyone else. My father's strong moral guidance, his refusal to let us slide when we made childhood mistakes like stealing matches or to let us skip our work on the farm, were a priceless education. The example he gave to us with the way he lived, whether it was with the hard work he exhibited every day just to support his family or the way he tried to work with everyone, even through the dangers of World War II and the bullying, angry German soldiers who could have ruined our lives at any moment, was perhaps the best lesson of all.

I have always taken the model my father set for me as a personal manifestation of God's love. When I faced temptation, whether it was from a beautiful woman or to gain extra profit by cutting corners in my business or the temptation to lash out in anger at those who had tried to hurt me, I always tried to let the light of God guide me. I tried always to remember that I was serving God's will, and it made those moments of difficulty easier to navigate.

I feel not only that I have the light of God's love with me but that he has sent angels to watch over me, including my father. And I, in turn, have tried to live my life in a way that reflects that light back out for others to see, and to follow if they wish. It is the way we humans can personally pass on the light of God's love: by allowing Him to shine through us for the benefit of everyone.

Finally, it felt like my family was where it should be. In the past I had always felt like something was going on behind my back or that there was something affecting the way my family felt and thought, something I never knew about. But now that had all changed, and things felt good.

Maria and I hadn't been to Italy in a few years, and all the while Gabriella had been talking to us about taking a trip, but not just any trip. We started talking about taking everyone—our kids, their spouses and all the grandchildren. It was quite an undertaking and even though it was something we wanted to do it took years to become reality.

But finally, we decided to go ahead. We started getting organized and planning in November, deciding where we would go and what we would do, and how we would accomplish the minor miracle of bringing eighteen people, including all those kids, on such a trip.

After months of talking and researching and planning, we left on July 14, 2007. I didn't think we could all fit together in one plane, but it turned out not to be a problem. However, the flight to Italy was nothing I'd like to remember. The turbulence was so bad that the plane shook violently for some fifteen or twenty minutes, with the pilots ordering everyone to take their seats.

It was like that for three or four hours, with a pretty good shake rattling the plane every minute or two. I have to admit it made me a little nervous. I looked around that plane and saw all the people whom I loved—my wife, my kids, my ten grandkids—and I was worried about what might happen. But turbulence is just turbulence after all, and the end of the flight was as smooth as it could be, paving the way for an ideal trip.

The first stop on my family's adventure was Venice and when we arrived I saw my nephew there waiting for us. He was to be our tour guide, in a sense, and was going to drive us around in a bus we had rented. Instead of the twenty-five-seater we'd planned for, there was a fifty-two-seat bus waiting for us. It was shiny and new, straight from the factory in Turkey, and it was the first time the bus had ever been used. It was quite impressive.

But in Venice especially, those buses can't go everywhere, and my nephew could only drive us so far before we had to get out and walk to the hotel, a forty-five-minute stroll along the canals.

Everyone else went sightseeing, but I had felt my age on that long walk, carrying my luggage like that. I stayed in and later on we all went to San Marco Square. And every shake of the turbulent plane or ache I felt suddenly became worth it as I watched our young grandchildren running around giggling and delightedly, chasing after the pigeons there. My little grandson, Michael, even caught one.

We spent the day walking around the city, trying to find a restaurant that would be able to seat the family together, taking in the beauty of Venice as best we could with the jet lag and time difference weighing us down. We hopped on a ferry that sped through the canals, pulling up at a stop right next to the hotel, which had many restaurants nearby with all the waiters out front calling out and urging people to come inside.

The next morning we headed for Florence, where we met up with another of my nephews, one I hadn't seen in ten years. I had never even met his wife. They came speeding up on a little Vespa and we all gathered at a big restaurant with a great buffet. The food was good and served fast, and it impressed my children and grandchildren. The little ones would look at Maria and tell her, "It's almost as good as the food you make, Nonna."

The family had a wonderful few days of sightseeing in Florence with many museums and famous paintings and sculptures to see, including the work of Michelangelo and da Vinci. There were a lot of long lines to wait on but it was worth it, especially for my son-in-law, who is a sculptor himself. We ate in a lovely *trattoria* that served homemade wine and at night the young people all went walking or got ice cream for the kids. I let the younger ones do most of the touring and wasn't afraid to spend my time resting or napping in the summer air.

After Florence we arrived in Marche, a region in central Italy where all of my wife's family is. The region is famous as the birthplace of the Italian saint Maria Goretti.

Our arrival at Maria's relatives' home was like a scene out of a movie. We pulled up to the front yard in that big bus, and my wife's whole family came running out of the house to greet us. We had such a good time—even my grandsons, who tried so hard to talk to their beautiful teenage cousins but couldn't because of the language barrier. There was a big feast, and we visited relatives of my father-in-law as well before we moved on.

It was sad to leave them, but we did, moving on to Rome. Our hotel was just two blocks from the Basilica of Santa Maria Maggiore, which is one of the largest churches in Rome. It was a lovely time; Maria and I would wake up early in the morning and go to a little shop behind the Basilica, where we would have cappuccino and some time for ourselves in the country where we'd met and fallen in love.

We made sure to see the Vatican and the Sistine

Chapel. My nephew, who continued to act as our tour guide, brought us to a huge restaurant—I had never seen anything like it. There were three floors to the eatery and thousands of people. The waiters brought out more food than one could have imagined—rigatoni, all kinds of pasta, and a twelve-inch pizza pie for each of my grandchildren. The food was so plentiful and good, and given with such generosity, it was like it didn't cost anything!

My nephew then took us to see all the places where the kings had lived, including Caesar and Nero. On our last morning in Rome, we had a stunning view of the city and got to really take in how big and beautiful it is. It was a moment I wouldn't trade for anything, looking out over Rome with those most precious to me by my side.

One of our last stops was Piglio, where I'd been born and raised, where I'd worked the farm alongside my parents and siblings, where my grandfather had teased and taught us, where I had been wowed and dismayed by the bombs and dogfights of World War II. The land was still in my family, in a manner of speaking, as it now belonged to relatives of my father.

It had been sixty years since I'd left Piglio, but people there still remembered me. It was one of the most joyous times of my life. My relatives prepared a beautiful feast to celebrate our visit, and it is an event I will never forget.

There was also a special ceremony wherein the mayor came to greet us, and I was presented with a nice plaque of congratulations for all I had achieved. The year before, when my cousin had been visiting us in Pennsylvania, he had taken note of all the things I had done—the homes I had built and the ceremony in which I was honored by the Italian-American society. He had taken a picture of that plaque and all kinds of other photographs of the homes I was building and the work I had undertaken. Little did I know that he'd brought all those pictures home to Piglio and showed everyone there what I was doing in America.

So this feast was something very special to me. It is always special and humbling when someone takes the time to recognize your work and your accomplishments, but to see an entire community turn out to do so, with such care and effort in a place that meant so much to me, was unbelievably touching.

But, as always, it was more than the pomp and circumstance that made the day memorable. Even more important than the plaque and the congratulations were the people who were there. After the ceremony there was a large group of us who went to a nearby restaurant. The restaurant was in an older building that had been remodeled and could only accommodate about fifty people—but oh, how I wish that place was bigger.

If God's love could be measured in any way, seen

in anything tangible on this Earth, it is certainly in the beauty of nature. Can anything compare with the bluest of skies, the boldest of flowers, the bounty of fruits and vegetables Mother Nature has to offer?

But perhaps God's most gorgeous example of His work, the best vehicle for the nurturing, nourishing light of His love, can be found in a much more accessible place. Maybe the way we can best feel God's glory is by basking in those most precious to us—those whom we know and love.

Looking around that restaurant, I saw those I had built my life around: my Maria, our children, my energetic, happy grandchildren. They were at once my present and my future. And I saw so much more.

The best parts of my past were on hand as well, including the love I had known all my life shining in the faces of three of my father's sisters, all either in their late eighties or early nineties. It was as if all the memories of my youth were colliding, in the happiest way I could ever imagine, with the life I had made.

It was a magical evening, one that had to end eventually but one that will live on in my heart as a golden memory. We then spent some time on the farm in Piglio, walking the same long road that my mother had taken to sell her vegetables, carrying her basket of food high on her head.

We spent a few hours there, my kids and grandkids taking some time to wander around the farm I'd grown up on, seeing the fruit trees and the mountains, the house. It was so special to see the family I worked so hard for and loved so much discovering the magical hillsides of my youth.

After our visit to Piglio we moved on to Lavinio, where the rest of my brothers and sisters were. I made sure my siblings knew that while we certainly wanted to spend time with them, what my family really wanted to do was enjoy some time on the beach while we were so close to it. We would visit with them later in the day, I assured them.

We headed down to the beach, to bask in the sun and the sight of the ocean, and before we knew it, my sisters and their daughters had brought a big table down to where we were, setting it up on the sand and filling it with such a bounty of food it was almost too much to be believed. There were figs, prosciutto, cheese made just that morning and salami that was so fresh, it had a wonderful taste. It was another amazing morning of food, fun and family.

Before our ten days in Italy ran out, there was one more special event. I told my brothers and sisters to gather all the close relatives and friends of ours from the neighborhood, from school, even those I might have forgotten, and invite them all to one more dinner.

And oh, what a dinner it was. There were about 100 people there at the restaurant in our hotel. I wanted to host the dinner as a way to give back to all the people who had been so generous to us, and as a way to celebrate our trip. I also wanted to show off the family I loved so much and worked so hard for. I wanted everyone at home in Italy to see my beautiful kids and grandchildren. It was a night of such happiness, togetherness and peace.

But just like that, before we knew it, the ten days were over and the trip we had spent so much time and energy planning was done.

One by one my kids and their spouses and families had to go, and each part of my family branched off to head their separate ways. Some went home, some continued traveling, while Maria and I stayed on a little longer in Italy.

The years of my life have gone by and I look around at all that I have accomplished, and I start to think about the future. I think about my kids and their families and what I can do to help them out. I think about what to do with Countryside Heights, which still has a significant number of lots left to develop despite all the work we have done there.

I have been semi-retired, taking it easy somewhat, not working as hard as I used to. But there is a lot of work left to do at Countryside Heights and I don't think it's fair to leave it completely in the hands of others, especially my kids. So I'm working with an engineer to get approval to develop the last sixty-one acres. Out of that acreage, we can create 100 lots, and that's what

I'm going to leave to my kids. They can divide the lots among themselves; they can sell them if they choose. And if they decide to sell the land for homes to be constructed, that is something I am confident that my daughters can rely on David to handle.

Sometimes, I feel the years weighing on me. Developing the rest of Countryside Heights, that is a six-, maybe eight-month job and I think I can handle that. Then I can spend my time relaxing, hunting, fishing and with Maria.

I look back on my life and think, *How the hell did I do all of this? How did I buy these properties, build these homes, build this business? How was I able to get all this done?* Because if I'd felt like this back then, I wouldn't have gotten anything done.

But when I consider my life's work, I know that my business is different than a lot of others. It's not like a hardware store, where you get up every morning and go open up and sell things. To be sure, that is good work. But my work is different.

To be a builder or a developer takes a different kind of thinking. It requires a long-term investment, a passion. You have to be willing to look into the future and plan, and be willing to see the possibilities in a piece of land even when there's nothing there yet. You have to be willing to take a chance, to work hard and give it everything you have.

I spent so much time as a teenager worrying about

my lack of education and wondering what I would do with my life but looking back, it seems to me that I was born for this work. To me, it wasn't really about making money above all else. It was about doing good work and creating good homes for people.

It was also about living and working in a way that valued good things and good people, and not living selfishly. It was about living in the pleasure of God, about doing what was right no matter what.

Everything that has happened to me, from working the farm in Piglio to coming to America to fighting the temptations put before me to not giving in to the malicious intentions of others, has been an example of how tough it can be to live for God.

All my life, it seemed that people underestimated me or had no faith in me. My own family in Italy had thought I was good for nothing more than eating; my own mother had worried about how I would do in America. From the start people had thought that because I didn't speak out or talk a lot, I was someone who could be ignored.

No matter how hard I tried there were always people looking to hurt me, thinking the worst of me or trying to derail me, even though I never did anything to anyone. I always tried to follow the advice of the one person who had always believed in me. My father's wise advice to focus on myself, worry about my own work and not be distracted by the small problems and missteps of others was so true, and was key to my achievements.

I was not and am not a perfect man. I have made mistakes just as any human being would. But I always thought I had beaten the evil that seemed to follow me. I thought putting my faith in God meant that I had some protection, some shield from the Devil's work. But in fact the problems and the pain were always there—sometimes prominently, sometimes working in the background. It is not something that can be gotten rid of or eliminated.

For all the deception that has haunted my life, there has been an equally strong presence of good, of God, to help me battle through. I feel that God has given me a gift, a spirituality that has manifested itself in ways that have helped me through my darkest times.

It is a lesson that some people never learn or never have enough faith to believe in. The idea that there is a force of good in this world, a force that faith gives us the key to unlock, is alien to most people, and that is a shame.

It is not natural for humanity to be so dark, to not be able to hold on to its faith. Just like the beauty of Mother Nature, it is natural for our goodness to bloom under the nourishing light of God. But so many have a hard time seeing it. People seem to think that if they cannot see an example of God's love before them, that He must not exist, or He must not be powerful enough to help them.

God's love is everywhere, but too often people get in their own way or cannot open their own eyes to see it. But it is all around us. In the blue of the sky, in the flowers and trees. God's love is in the love of our families, the eyes of our children, the faith and partnership of our spouses.

Sometimes, God shows His most faithful a more tangible sign of his power. He sent guardians to help me as I became stuck in a tug of war between the good and evil of the world. The greatest of these has been my father who, when he was alive, never failed to teach me the lessons I needed to learn and had faith in me even when I was a tiny boy playing in the sand.

But the power of God is such that even years after my father's death, he came to me often, visiting me in my dreams when I needed help and confidence the most. Appearing before me at my darkest hour of temptation to remind me of the promise I'd made years earlier that had defined my life: to serve God's will.

There were so many of God's troops looking out for me, including the family friend who had appeared before me, years after her death, to apologize for insulting me, or the beautiful, precious son with whom we had fifteen years of life and laughter.

In my worst hour, when I thought I had lost my

family to vicious lies, I thought I had lost everything. But in that moment, Jesus himself appeared before me to remind me that my situation was not as bad as I thought.

I have worked hard, worked until I was physically exhausted, working two and three jobs so that I could give my family and my dreams security. I have done what I could to treat people the right way, to do business in a way that was driven by what was morally right, by what God would have wanted rather than by profit.

And my faith has been rewarded. I have worked hard and have a successful business beyond what anyone who knew me as a child could have imagined. The homes I have spent my life building are known for their quality and are even today well-regarded by those who have bought them. I, a man with a fifth-grade education, was able to earn my GED.

I have been given experiences and opportunities few others get, whether they were good jobs or the chance to make dreams into reality, like purchasing the farm out of which I made Countryside Heights, or being able to bring my mother to America at one of my most successful hours, or taking my whole family home to Italy.

I have seen many couples who raise children only to see those children scatter themselves across the country and forgo their closest relationships with parents and siblings. But my family, my most precious asset, has always been loving and close, and once we were able to weed out the dark insinuations that had dampened its spirit, our family became stronger than ever.

There has always been a group of angels watching over me, helping me make the right choices. I feel as though this is the ultimate gift that God has given me, and that I have a responsibility to tell the world about the power of God's love. People should know how close God is, how He walks with us every day.

As it says in the Bible, the power of God's love is like a light, like the sun that shines down over everything. It is a light we all have access to, one that every person can open themselves to—some more than others. I have read it in the Bible, and it has always stayed with me. If you have a light, you don't hide it under the bed where no one can see it. If you have a light, you hold it up high so that it shines for everyone.

Even to the death fight for truth,
and the Lord your God will battle for you.
Sirach 4:28 (Saint Joseph Edition)

They have set a trap for my feet; my soul is bowed down;
They have dug a pit before me, May they fall into it themselves!
Psalms 57:7 (Saint Joseph Edition)

About the Author

David Beato is currently a well-known real estate developer in southwestern Pennsylvania, where he lives with his wife. He has one son and two daughters who are all college educated and married, and his greatest joy is spending time with his children and grandchildren.